MW00623822

BECOMING
JULIE

A MEMOIR

Julie Paisley

BECOMING JULIE
A MEMOIR

Copyright © 2023 by Julie Paisley

Front Page photo by Hannah Diane Photography
Back page photo by Abby Grace Photography

To request permissions, contact the publisher at
publish@joapublishing.com or julie@juliepaisley.com.

Hardcover ISBN: 978-1-961098-13-8
Paperback ISBN: 978-1-961098-11-4
eBook ISBN: 978-1-961098-12-1
Printed in the USA.

Joan of Arc Publishing
Meridian, ID 83646
www.joapublishing.com

TABLE OF CONTENTS

BECOMING JULIE

INTRODUCTION

Well, hello there, Friend!

If you care enough to open this book and read my story, I already consider you to be my friend. Whether you somehow found your way to my book, or my book found its way to you, we'll just chalk it up as some kind of inspired destiny and that we were meant to know each other. So, now that we are officially acquainted, get that guest room ready because by the time you finish reading this book, we will most certainly be friends. I mean, I'll have just shared my heart with you and it's time for a hug. I'm pretty low maintenance—I'm even fine with sleeping on the couch! My only request is a cold coke in the morning.

Truly, I am so happy you decided to pick up this book and read my story, thus making us friends. I hope that you are, at least, some kind of fan of Disney, like I am. Well, alright, I'm a BIG fan. Let's face it, Disney is pretty much my happy place. Walt Disney World and I share a birthday year and I was born in the same state (yay Florida) so perhaps I was destined to be a Disney fan. If you are not, go ahead and just keep that little detail to yourself, and don't let me know. Okay?

Anyway, I'm sure you must have your own personal top picks amongst all the Disney films. There are plenty to choose from. But for me, one of my absolute favorites is *Finding*

Nemo, and I can pretty much quote it by heart. One of my favorite parts of the movie is when Dory finds herself with the sharks and she introduces herself to those critical carnivores. So here I go, trying to introduce myself to people who don't necessarily "know" me, but who I already consider to be my friend, in the best true-Dory fashion I can present:

"Hi, I'm Julie. Fish are friends and I don't like seafood so I really don't eat them."

See how easily we became friends?

In the first few paragraphs you learned that:

1. I love a coke in the morning instead of coffee.
2. I love Disney.
3. One of my favorite movies is *Finding Nemo*.
4. Walt Disney World Magic Kingdom and I share a birthday year.
5. I don't like seafood.

I think that's a pretty good start. So, here we go!

A LITTLE BACKSTORY...

For those of you who grew up with me in my small town, you know me as "Julie from Yulee," or possibly as "Ju-Ju" or "Jules." Or even as "Robert Hinson's daughter," "Little Julie," "The Sensitive One," "The One That Cries If You Look at Her Wrong," "The Overachiever," "The One We Called Flounder," and more recently, you might refer to me as "The One Who Came from a Small Town, Is Now a Famous Photographer, and Is Waaaay Too Expensive." Somehow you've also probably convinced yourself that I'm a millionaire. (I'm not, by the way. Sorry to burst that bubble.)

For those of you who I went to college with, you know me as the one who was in ensemble and sang on TV, the one who was in plays and musicals, and the dormitory building floor-leader who pulled the fire alarm in Dixon Tower, sending everyone into a panic as the fire department responded, all because the exhaust fans brought in smoke from a nearby neighbor burning trash.

And yes, I was also the one in a number of promo brochures, photographed sitting with my future husband, who, at the time of the photo, was dating one of my best friends. I was also the campus tour guide who was annoyingly too happy all the time. And I was the one whose ensemble uniform was the loud floral dress with the huge polka dot collar and massive bow that would move every time I took a deep breath to sing. (Please don't judge me here—it was the early 90s and I had the hair to match.)

Finally, for those of you who have known me in my photography years, you know me as a fine art wedding photographer who has been published in numerous blogs and wedding magazines, a celebrity photographer with photo-covers for *People* magazine, a world traveler, someone who speaks on stages and owns her own photography conference, and blah, blah, blah. You see me as successful, high-achieving, what others might call "goals," making a ton of money, with a perfect marriage, perfect children, and a perfect life.

Okay, I think I'll stop with the lists now because you may sense that there is a plot twist coming. And there is. You'll see. But before I get into the upcoming nitty-gritty, here are just a couple little points to re-center the dial.

My story is about all the good *and* all the bad. And I'm really glad you're here because we all need friends to share our struggles with. Maybe you just picked up this book because it looked interesting or somehow caught your eye. Or maybe a friend let you borrow it and urged you to read it. Maybe it fell out of the sky and landed on your doorstep. In any event, I'm glad you are here. All the good and all the bad are forthcoming. And since I already consider you my friend, you need to be aware that I'm also a big-time *hugger*. And throughout this book, you'll undoubtedly find places where I'm welling up with tears from all the emotions I went through. But you'll see that I keep on going because I just have to get it all out and into the arms of a friend so we can cry together. That is how I will silently ask for, and give, hugs throughout this story. So, there you go—you have been warned, new friend.

I think that's enough background as I start getting into the not-so-perfect side of things. And yes, in case you are wondering, I truly have been all those things mentioned already. Except the perfect part. I'm sooooooo far from perfect. You could call it galaxies or even universes away. *But I am better than I was.* Because in all truthfulness, I have discovered that the "previous me" from the past is not *who*, or even *what*, defines the person I really am today. That previous person, who I'll call her a "stranger I remember well," is grown and gone. Galaxies away in another direction.

To be honest, we all have learned to be chameleons in order to survive. And I, like so many of you, grew up into a life of people-pleasing, and was only concerned with what other people thought of me. I grew into the feeling, or more accurately the "belief," (which I am guilty of nurturing for years upon years), that I was only valuable when I was successful in the eyes of others. But what about me? Julie? Oh, she's just the person in the mirror. My reflection doesn't have thoughts or feelings, so why would I listen to her? If I go away, she goes away, but all these other people are still around telling me what they want.

Yes, I'm admitting to the entire world that I spent nearly fifty years living life as an imposter. And that is why they say that life is a stage. I would know that because I've been a performer on that stage for almost my entire life. And if you were to dig down deep and have a conversation with your heart of hearts, you would likely admit that so have you. So, before you judge me, read *all* of this book, and I'm sure you will see yourself on the same map that I did.

I guess I will never fully understand why we live in a world where it's so difficult to learn how to just be ourselves. Why are we conditioned, from the time we are born, to be the person that someone else has envisioned for us? Whether it's religion, birth order, gender, or environment, there are always rules and protocols that are forcefully strapped on to us at a very early age. It's just crazy to me how when we are mere toddlers, the adults in our lives already have our lives and personalities planned out before we can even say our first words. It reminds me of a verse from an old Cat Stevens song where he says, "From the moment I could talk, I was ordered to listen." It's a commentary on the false framework children are born into, as well as the challenges they face while growing up. So, it may not be *intrinsically* our fault. But later on, we start becoming more mentally and emotionally independent and we begin to see ourselves differently from what others expect of us. And if we don't notice that we are walking down a path that someone else chose for us, that path becomes our trap, our daily-deception, and therefore our responsibility to find a way to save ourselves.

If you have ever met me, or have been following me on social media, you would never believe that originally my personality was that of a rather shy child, who was literally afraid of people. I would entertain myself for hours in my room with my dolls and books, and I was *not* the chatty life of the party. I loved to listen to music on my record player and just dream. And I didn't mind doing it all alone. In fact, being alone with my imagination was my thing, my groove, my sanctuary.

But somehow, by the time I was nine, with whatever cocktail of influences were bestowed upon me by those that I believed had my best interests in mind, I became convinced that whoever I truly was, simply was not good enough to be happy on my own. Maybe I allowed too much in. Maybe the voices of the adults in my life were louder than my own thoughts. I dunno, maybe it was something else altogether. But whatever the case was, I ended up believing that the more I did, achieved, and accomplished would cover up that shy little girl who just wanted to sit in a room and read all the time. And even though I was following orders and performing on command, the timid and self-conscious me was still hidden inside. And yes, I had come out of my "shell" quite a bit on the surface, but this only meant that I was now openly exposed to criticism, which is what I really didn't want. I would cry and beg to not have to sing or perform in front of people because, deep down, I actually didn't like the attention.

It was this exposure that made me feel the sadness in thinking that people would only like me if I followed orders and did all the things for all the people. I thought, "Yes. *The Perfect One* is who I need to be. That is the girl that everyone will like." So, I faked it. And then, soon enough, even I started believing the lie and The Real Julie got buried deeper and deeper under the commands and expectations of the adults in my life. Fast forward 42 years, and at least now I am able to pinpoint that this was where my life-long obsession with perfectionism, people-pleasing, and living a life on the receiving end of somebody else's puppet strings began. All in that shy, little 9-year-old girl. How I wish I could go back and give her a hug and tell her that just being JULIE was enough. I would never have gotten to what would become the lowest and most horrifying moment of my life. But then again, if I were able to pull that time-traveling stunt off, I also wouldn't have gotten to the point of writing this very book that you are now reading that will hopefully change your life.

I guess it comes down to realizations. The sooner we understand that life doesn't happen TO us, it happens FOR us, the better off we all will be. Because deep down, all of us can relate to insecurities. At some point, we all believe the lie that we can never, *ever* show anyone the damaged or broken parts of ourselves that just naturally come with living in an imperfect world.

And to be honest, I believed the lie and felt that I was predestined to be great. I could never be "average." Not *me*. No. No. Nooooooo. After all, I was the firstborn of three girls. I was the first grandchild on both sides and they literally called me "Princess" waaaay too often. It's a wonder I didn't develop a complex of some kind, for Pete's sake. Oh, but wait a second there because, actually, I did. But I wouldn't know for a long time.

As a kid, I was always told that I was the pretty one, *so I had to be*. I was the talented one, *so I had to be*. I was the smart one, *so I had to be*. You get the idea. But honestly, and even more to the point, I had the fear of God so deeply ingrained in my head that if I didn't use my "God-given talents," He would take them away! And that simply would not do. So, from a very early age, I told myself that there was no room for failure. None. I was taught that "to whom much is given, much is expected." "It's just part of life," I told myself. "It's the luck of the draw," I lied to myself. "And since I was born this way, I'll just magically prevent any form of failure from entering my life, and The Real Julie will never know." I was so convinced that I had to be extraordinary that I didn't even see all those puppet strings attached, even though I never truly felt that my life was my own to live.

I was born in 1971 and life was different back then. Especially if you were raised in the south. Moreover, in a Baptist Church. I mean, really, can I get an amen? But looking back, I don't *blame* my parents or the church for pushing me. After all, that is what *they* were taught to do as well. If your child shows some real potential and talent, you do everything in your power to make sure they succeed. Truth be told, I even found myself doing this with my own children. It's a perpetuating cycle from one generation to another, and is just something parents do. But perhaps I just wish that I would have been strong enough to make my inner voice heard and convey what I wanted and needed for me. If I could have done that, they would have known that I didn't want to be only what others expected. It probably would have changed my outlook as a parent to some degree as well.

Speaking of growing up, on paper, and in my memories to be honest, I really did have a pretty perfect childhood. And yes, I know we all suffer a little as adults from generational and sometimes religious trauma, but when I look back over my childhood—dang, I had it pretty good.

I grew up with a hard-working, loving, and Godly dad. My dad was, and still is, one of the most generous people I've ever known. I can't tell you how many times I saw him give everything in his wallet to a person in need and he ALWAYS took care of us. I know there were times growing up when life was hard, but he made sure we girls never knew it.

My mother was that "Betty Crocker" type of mom who loved her husband and her children, and never missed out on anything we were a part of. She was always there for us, and we three girls were her life. I never, ever, even for a moment, wondered if my parents loved me. And I cannot remember a time where I didn't feel safe. In fact, and I know it's maybe a little weird, but they still make me feel safe, and I'm 51 years old.

Seriously, my parents are some of the best people I know. Of course, they are not perfect. And sure, they made mistakes because, let's face it, who doesn't? But my goodness, I hit the jackpot when it comes to family.

I grew up in a church that felt like family. We affectionately called pretty much everyone "Aunt" and "Uncle." I know what you are thinking: "What kind of strange cult did this girl grow up in?" Yes, it may seem strange by today's standards, but you have to remember that I grew up in the 70s and 80s, and life was different then. It's just what you did in a small town where you knew everybody.

Our church, like so many in the south at the time, also had its own private Christian school. It's so rare these days, but I started kindergarten there and also graduated from the same school at 17. In fact, my senior class consisted of a whopping ten students. And out of those ten graduates, five of us started kindergarten together and stayed together all the way through the 12th grade. If you want, you can call me a freakin' unicorn for living my best fairytale life, because it was almost reminiscent of *Little House on the Prairie*. At least, that's how I remember it. It wasn't perfect but I'm thankful I never saw that until I became an adult. Because despite it all, my childhood memories are really magical.

Anyway, to continue on about the family dynamics, both of my parents were born into large families. I had grandparents that adored me and were my best friends, and there were loads of aunts, uncles, and cousins who I saw on a weekly basis. We had big family get-togethers often. There was just so much love and laughter. In fact, both sides of my family were all close friends with each other, and it wasn't uncommon to have both grandmothers and a few aunts and uncles present at every family event.

I grew up in a house that was small, but was always packed to the rim with all of my friends. We had slumber parties on weekends, as well as what seemed like all summer long. Ahhhh yes, those were the days when it wasn't scary to let your children stay overnight at someone else's home. We didn't just sit around and watch movies, and there were no cell phones. Instead, we played and played and played. We played board games seemingly endlessly, swam until we had turned into prunes, played dress-up and held beauty pageants for my mom and her friends to be judges for. We also put on impromptu plays that had no plot but made all the sense in the world to us. I remember when my dad had to work nights, my mom would warn him to be careful when he came home because he would have to step over the bodies sleeping all over the living room floor. Those were the good old days. Have you seen the movie *The Truman Show*? That was pretty much my life as a youngster.

But Friend, if you haven't figured it out yet, this thing we call *life* is far from perfect. You can probably even see the expression on my face changing right now as I am getting closer to the time that the magic bubble burst, bringing my perfect fairytale to a halt when I was 15 years old. And you know what? Everything that has happened to me in the past 36 years since then has formed me into the person I am right now, sitting here, writing my story so that I can help others. It took me 50 years to get here, and my prayer is that it won't take you that long.

I am presenting this book in two parts. Part one is *The Hard* and part two is *The Healing*. And as much as we would like to skip to the good part, like all the viral TikToks out there, that's just not real life, folks. Reality sucks sometimes, and we can't just cover up the hard and wish it all away while expecting our "happily ever after" to roll across some virtual screen in our heads.

I understand that the first part of my story may be triggering for some. But just remember that there is hope, and all the hard has brought me to where I am today. I *am* healing. I *am* changed. And I have written this book to prove it. Also, I understand that many, if not most people, would want to keep their story to themselves because they are too scared to share it, revealing truths that might show others their weaknesses or their demons. But for me, I'm too scared to NOT share it.

2021 changed everything for me and I am calling it my "awakening." You will read in the first part of this book that I had gone through hard times before, but that year would shake me down to my very core. And if not for the grace of God, things could be so different right now and this book would not be in your hands. So, I need to warn you, if you are reading this book because you think it's going to show a life of rainbows and unicorns, or some Disney magic like the cover lets you assume, you might want to put it down. Or you can put on your big-girl panties and realize that life is FAR from perfect. That *you* are far from perfect. That bad things happen to good people and it's not a punishment for sin or something bad we are doing in our life. Sometimes, it is just realizing that bad things don't happen TO us, they happen FOR us. And in the end, we are better people for it because those are the parts of life that build us into stronger, better versions of who we are.

So, if you have lived a life of people-pleasing, or unfair comparison, and are feeling like you can never be enough by just being you, then you need to finish reading this. Even if it triggers you, keep reading to the end.

The story you are reading is really just a bunch of smaller stories. My stories. And I know them well because I lived them. And although you and I have lived different lives, comprised of very different events, I'm sure you will be able to relate in some meaningful way. Despite the differences we have in the accounts of our lives, we have more in common than most people ever even try to consider. We all came into this world the same way. We all start out as innocent babies who all have an undiscovered purpose. We are all just a compilation of stories. Some good, and others not so good. We all cry, laugh, eat, breathe, sleep, need, want, suffer, win, fail, find, lose, grow, hurt, disappoint, hope, and love, just to name a few things we already have in common.

And this book is just that; it's my real life. It's going to make you laugh, cry, and nod your head as you read because you see in these stories a common thread that runs through your life. I'm nothing special. Or perhaps, more accurately, you are just as special as I am. And that is encouraging for us both. We are all born the same. No matter our background or how we were raised, we all have one thing in common. WE ARE HUMAN.

My prayer for this book is that you realize you ARE enough by just being you. And all of your accomplishments, trophies, and success are just brief mentions on social media, which are really just marks on an invisible sheet of paper that few people ever read. They do not define who we are. Those things are bonuses, and while they do have their momentary significance, they do not carry water on their own, and wouldn't ever exist without YOU. You are the underlying thing of value, and yes, *you are enough*. But there is no guidebook or instruction manual to all of this, or any of this. In God's eyes, we are all precious. He loves us just the way we are, and it's sad that we forget that. There is no checklist of physical actions to tick off to be deemed "worthy" when we die, only that we give our heart to Him.

And yeah, I do love Jesus. If you don't share the same passion for Him, that is your decision, not mine. We can agree to disagree and I will still love you. But I politely ask you, please *don't assume* anything about me in advance. Please don't wrongly "assign" me to a place somewhere in the stereotypical realm of perception on how a religious person is viewed in today's world. That wouldn't be fair to either of us. My view of organized religion has changed over the years. I have no space for judgmental Christians in my life and I'm certainly not one of them.

So, no matter where your beliefs fall, I know I can help you. I'm not here to push my beliefs on you. That is not what this book is about. I truly believe that we can live in harmony with each other, and that it is actually healthy for us to NOT agree on everything. I believe that we should live our lives with a mutual respect for each other, because again, we are ALL human. I believe that we all should love like Jesus does, and that is how I try to live my life.

So, to end this introduction, EVERYONE is welcome here in this space and I just wanted you to know where I stand.

PART 1

THE HARD

"Sometimes we just have to STOP in order to START OVER, because SLOWING DOWN has already expired."

Julie Paisley

PART 1:
CHAPTER 1

"C" WORDS

DEEP BREATH

Here we go.

Like I said earlier, I'm not going to start this book with sunshine and rainbows. I mean, if that is how my life is all the time, why would I be here putting *work* into writing a book to help others in the first place? Kinda defeats the purpose, right?

I mean, who would want to pick up and read a book written by someone who wants *you* to accept the imperfect and stop the cycle of people-pleasing and comparison, but not have any firsthand experience in dealing with those things on her own. What kind of heroine would that be?

If that's the case, I recommend that you take this book back to where you bought it from and ask for a refund. Because the truth is, Friend, we learn from the hard events in life, and the rainbows never come until after the storm. I'm going to be honest with you right now—if you have so far been spared from any "hard" in your life, you are either a unicorn, living in denial, or it's just not your time yet.

Because that perfect life disappeared when Eve ate the forbidden fruit.

This book is NOT about how great I am, nor about my accomplishments. Nope. It's quite the opposite. And of course, if you spend any time at all online, you have surely noticed that we humans have become really good at displaying only our highlight reels and creating a visual narrative of the story we want the world to see. It's image advertising at its best (or worst, depending on how you look at it). And I would know, I didn't become the president of the "look at me" club just to make my parents proud. Nope, I'm starting this book at the lowest time ever in my life because, at least that way, it can only go up from there. And I've always thought it's important to be able to find the silver lining sometimes.

Now remember, I warned you, and told you to put your big girl panties on. Also, if you can make it through this first part of the book, the rest of the hard stories I share will seem like a birthday party with the biggest bounce house ever. And cake. Lots of cake.

But, before you get all sensitive, I will tell you that, as of right now, assuming that nothing crazy has happened to me since I finished writing this book, there *is* a happy ending. There is an underlying purpose for me in writing about the "hard" in my life. And the ultimate goal is to prevent you from making the same mistakes that I did. I don't want anyone to ever get to the place where I was in my story that almost killed me. And if not for the saving grace of God, I would not be here today. Because on November 9, 2021, I was on my knees, alone in a bathroom, with a whole bunch of sleeping pills in my hand, a lifetime of confused emotions running through my veins, crying my eyes out, and convulsing with fear and indecision as I was contemplating how my life would be easier if I was no longer in it.

Very few people that I've ever known are aware of this fact, and I'm holding my breath right now because of all the potential text messages that could start coming in now that I've spilled the beans with this confession. It's not something I'm proud of, and it's not something that I even wanted to put out in the world. But as I said earlier, I'm too afraid to NOT share it. That moment was, by far, the lowest point in my life because I was literally only seconds away from following through with all of those pills only inches away from being ingested. And since I have confessed this much, I should come completely clean and tell you that although this was the closest I came to removing myself from all future chapters, it wasn't the first time that I had thought about ending my life.

Let me reflect for a moment. I am what you could call a "sensitive soul." There are various other legitimate, psychological labels and descriptions for this type of person, and maybe I'll get into that more at a later time. But for now, let's suffice and sum up with "empath." An empath is one who not only *can* feel others' pain, but *does* feel others' pain, day in and day out. And because life can be so difficult sometimes, those of us with sensitive souls feel it all so much harder than the rest of the world. It's both a blessing and a curse to care so deeply, but we will come back to all of that later.

I do want to make something very clear to you though. This book is not about doom and gloom. No, it's quite the opposite. However, before you can appreciate worldly joy and inner peace, you need to have a genuine understanding of how significant the darker moments affect your overall perception, which, in turn, affects your physiology and also your spirit. And if this collection of pages is going to inspire lives and help people through some of that darkness, then I'm going to have to be completely honest with you. There is no sugar coating. I'm called to speak my truth and that is exactly what I will do.

And when it matters most, we find that the truth is hard. As humans, we tend to have our guard up most of the time. We don't want to hear or even acknowledge the truth because we are walking down some uncomfortable path, and if we can't do it with style, we choose to omit its importance from our thoughts. No one wants to appear to be weak or broken to others, or especially to themselves. So, naturally, we remove those scenes from our highlight reels. We try to forget them altogether because once we forget something, we conveniently don't even have to admit that we were ever there in the first place.

I know, because that's how I handled it. I found out at an early age that people don't want to hear about the hard. People like pretty. People like shiny things. People like perfection. So that's what they want to portray. And the cycle continues until it stops, and then it's too late. Because walking in the dark is like trespassing. That's where you realize you are walking down somebody else's chosen path, and you've likely been there most or even all of your life. That's the trap. That's the daily deception. And when you realize it's too late, the trap has already sprung. So don't let it get to that point. Yes, I know, that's far easier said than done, but in reality, *what isn't?*

In my life, and especially since that night in November of 2021, I have learned that good and bad both exist together and it's normal. And most importantly, it's okay. While it *is* something that you must work on to come to grips with, it's okay, nonetheless. Recognizing that it's okay is proof that you've had a change in your perspective. And a change in perspective changes *everything.*

The year 2019 ended for me as one of my most successful years in my business, both on paper and in the eyes of others. Unless you know me personally, outside of what I've already told you here, you probably know little about me. We have all had something come across our path that captivated us in some way, for reasons we may not be able to fully explain. This happened to me in 2008 when I received an unexpected gift that changed my life as I knew it. That gift was a camera.

I do not have a degree, nor even a minimal background in photography. I graduated from college in 1993 with a degree in Music Education, and I looked forward to being a teacher, which I truly loved. At the time, I was teaching both kindergarten classes and music classes in the same private school that I graduated from. I lived in the same hometown that I grew up in, and we were raising our children in the same environment.

I was only two classes away from graduating with my Master's in Special Education and already had the rest of my life planned out. I can assure you that becoming a photographer was NOWHERE in my well-laid plans. But when I picked up that camera during my summer break from teaching, something stirred in me, and I was forever changed. By 2010, at the age of 37, not only had I retired from teaching, I also had a photography business that had quickly grown spectacularly well for the industry. By 2011, I was already a well-known photographer and considered a huge success.

By 2019, on the outside, I had a life that most people would envy. I had reasonable wealth and people knew my name. I had a big social media following and I had worked my way up to the luxury and celebrity wedding market, which in that world, means I had "made it." Yes, I was now a leader in my profession. I traveled the world and spoke on stages. I even taught other, more experienced photographers how to develop their craft. I was getting paid almost the same amount for one day of wedding photography that I was paid for an entire year of teaching. I lived on the high of accolades and my perfectly produced Instagram feed. My life was the envy of all.

My children had grown up to be good people. Mari-Kate was thriving as a young adult (I will share more of her story later) and Noah had just started his first year in college. My marriage was good, and I was able to retire my husband from his corporate job in 2011. We enjoyed a life of traveling and working together to continue building my photography business. I believed with false security that life was good, and I just knew that 2020 was going to be huge. Everything that I had worked for was finally coming true. And yet, despite the external signs of success, something was just "off." I couldn't quite put my finger on it. But it didn't matter how I felt (or didn't feel) on the inside. It was what people *saw* that was most important. 2020 was going to be MY YEAR. I was so sure of this that I even bought a sweatshirt with "2020" in sparkly letters on it so I could celebrate in advance.

At the start of that year, I had smiled so big in all of my online posts, and showed off my new Chanel and Gucci purses that I had just purchased on a recent trip to Paris. But Friend, I was dying on the inside. The pressures of *keeping up*, *showing up*, and then *living up* to this pretend perfect life had become paralyzing.

Now, you may be thinking to yourself, "Oh, you poor little thing. It's such a shame that you had it so good." But I didn't even recognize myself anymore. If I had to pick the exact word for it, I would say that it had become grotesque. Not gross, like when you see roadkill or something. There was a genuine *surrealness* to it. Almost like how a good thing is great in moderation, but horrible when you have too much. Right?

For example, I would bet that you love mashed potatoes and gravy on Thanksgiving. (If I'm wrong, please just work with me here and roll with it.) Now imagine that because you love mashed potatoes and gravy sooooooo much, your mom decides to treat you to a nice scoop of potatoes and a gallon of gravy. It's still mashed potatoes and gravy, right? But you can't even fathom trying to finish it because doing so would truly be grotesque, in the true sense of the word. You would certainly become ill if you ate it all, and you can't even get past the first few bites because it's too rich, too monotonous, too-filling-too-fast, too much "tadaaah" in the gravy and not enough of the basics from the potatoes (which you could probably eat until you are full if there were no gravy at all!).

That's what I mean by grotesque. My life had little of the basic necessities and way too much of the gravy. This bigger-than-life, online personality was so far removed from that shy, little 9-year-old girl. "Ughhh! What have I done?" is all I could think about sometimes. I had become a puppet going through the motions. But I was the only one who knew it.

After a while, I realized that I wasn't sleeping well, or at all sometimes. I worked constantly. Even when physically resting, because I knew I needed it, my mind was trying to be this "everything" to everybody. I couldn't enjoy my so-called rest. My health was horrible and my relationships were, at best, strained in some cases. The pressure to keep climbing when "you've made it" made me feel like if I stepped back, I would be the biggest failure on the planet. And that external, authoritative voice I'd been hearing my whole life told me, "People don't just walk away from what you have accomplished." So, I believed the lie again, and thought that if I let people know how I was really feeling, it would ruin everything.

"Keep climbing, Julie. This is what a person does. You made it. And with success comes sacrifice, so suck it up!" Oh, how the false narratives in my head would swarm and just take over in full control of my judgment.

I started the year with more anxiety than I had ever felt in my life. Every moment I felt like my life was a ticking time bomb. It's like I knew deep down that all hell was about to break loose and it would almost cost me everything.

I had set my business up so that the majority of my work for 2020 would be in Europe. I had epic weddings scheduled in places that I had only dreamed of. I had sold-out workshops abroad. The Hybrid Collective, a photography conference I started with some colleagues, was thriving and it was going to be our biggest year yet.

We were also supposed to build our forever dream home. Life was good, at least that is what everyone thought and what I told myself on a daily basis. But then, we all know what happened in March of 2020, and the world literally shut down.

None of us really saw that one coming, nor did we even imagine the path of destruction it would leave years later.

I don't think I had any idea how the impact of a global pandemic would change the trajectory of my life, but looking back on it now, I'm so glad it did. I'm sure you have heard the quote that says, "The only guarantees in life are taxes, weddings, and funerals." I'm not sure who said it first, or even if I'm saying it right, but you get the picture. As a wedding photographer, I believed I had the greatest job-security ever. Oh, but 2020 sure proved me wrong. And with that, all the wedding photographers of the world say, "Amen."

At first, I was like every other person who accepted the little break and time home with my family. It was almost fun. Lots of time to play games, watch movies, figure out the toilet paper situation—I welcomed that break. I liked sleeping in and not having to get dressed or go anywhere. It was the longest time I had spent at home without traveling in ten years, and for a little while, everything was fine.

Our big house on three acres of land in the country with a cute, little cottage that doubled as my office where I hosted retreats, had sold the year before and we were now living in a townhome temporarily (nearer to civilization, so hello DoorDash and Instacart) while searching for our forever home. Noah had started college in the fall, so downsizing was good, and honestly, I'm so thankful that we didn't have that big mortgage and other expenses from living in a big house in the middle of nowhere. It's almost crazy how God knew our needs before it even came to pass. However, when Noah had to leave his college campus due to COVID, in order to do his learning online, my husband, Matt, and I were also working from home. We did what we needed to in order to make it work, but let's just say that quarters were a little tight. We all became really close (literally), and for a family where each person needs personal space, I'm sure you can imagine how that turned out. I'm surprised we still love each other.

Honestly though, I thought this would all be over in a few months; I think we all did. And as we all know now, it wasn't. By the middle of the year, I realized that there would be no work for me for the rest of 2020.

And just like that, everything was suddenly different. Panic sank in, and my anxiety and depression absolutely knocked me over because I was now aware that I had been hit with a genuine triple-whammy. First, I was a destination photographer, but travel was now closed. Second, I was a wedding photographer, and weddings were now canceled in just about every country I would have been planning to visit. And third, I was an educator for other photographers, but even they were out of work; and they started cancelling their monthly subscriptions to my workshops and mentoring courses.

Skip forward a few crying sessions, and my monthly income now equaled precisely zero. But I was scrappy, and I was also really good at pretending, so I just started to do what I did best. I pivoted and I helped others do the same. We lived on our savings as best we could and I sold some of my travel prints. Somehow, we made enough money to survive, and I began telling myself that 2021 would be here soon and things would get back to normal. But once again, from the outside looking in, I appeared to be just fine, while deep down I was a wreck.

To others, I was the bubbly positive influence that my profession needed. I was regularly showing up online, doing everything I could to keep giving and giving to others. While, in reality, the deeper truth was nothing like that. I kept pouring into others' cups, but my own cup had become empty. Not even a drop of water left. It was bone dry.

Remember when I said earlier that life is a stage? Well guess what? During 2020 and 2021, I put my acting skills to work. And although I forced myself to be the star of the show, I'm kinda still wondering where my Oscar is.

Around August of 2020, we came to the sad realization that our hopes of moving into our dream home that year were not going to be fulfilled. We really didn't want to stay in the townhome, but financially it didn't feel like a smart time to buy another house and take a chance with real estate in a market which had gone CRAZY. We just needed to accept our predicament and find another solution that didn't seem so risky.

So, what did we do? Something totally crazy, of course! I still don't know what the tipping point was in our rationale. Call it the empty-nester syndrome, a midlife crisis, grasping at straws, or the ever-popular "it seemed like a good idea at the time" in order to try and make sense of how to deal with a world that was on fire, as well as societal collapse in a freefall. Whatever it was, though, it convinced us to do something a little nuts. So, we bought a 40-foot RV and a huge truck to pull it with. And just like that, Matt, Mari-Kate, and I, along with two dogs and a cat decided to head out on a grand adventure. It had been decided that we were going on the road for a year while the world calmed down.

Now, y'all, I really thought I was going to live the RV life wearing my *Love Shack Fancy* dresses while carrying my pink Chanel purse. I was going to re-invent the reel and this was going to be the bougie RV life for me. I imagined decorating a space that would be pinned all over Pinterest and people from all over the world would follow me. It had been decided and I had my heart set on it.

But there was this kind of big thing I didn't yet know. There is absolutely NOTHING bougie about living in an RV! And the people you come in contact with while traveling and living the RV life *could not even begin* to care less about what designer you were wearing.

And now, even today, as I work on these chapters, I look out my window to see that very same RV parked in our front yard. I can hear it mocking me as it talks to the breeze going by. I can hear it laughing at me, and sometimes I laugh along with it. Because actually, it wasn't all bad. And as crazy as it sounds, sometimes I miss it. It was the one action in my life that I've truly ever taken on an absolute whim. There was an element to it all that was just so freeing and liberating. And for the first time in my life, I could simply disappear without feeling like I had to be someone else.

Our adventure on the road started off great. We spent the fall of 2020 and the winter heading into 2021 traveling around the south and life was good. I'll admit that it was a bit of a tight squeeze for three humans plus our furry family members. But it did feel cozy, and I actually enjoyed tiny living.

Not having the pressure of owning a home, and all that goes with it, relieved a lot of stress since I really wasn't back to working full-time yet. We were not tied down to anything, and the freedom to just go wherever we wanted whenever we wanted was a very healing and inspiring dose of well-deserved medicine.

We spent a lot of time at Disney, as well as a great deal of time in Florida in general. Honestly, walking the beaches in January and February and feeling the warmth of the sunshine on my face was the best therapy imaginable, especially for someone who suffers from seasonal depression. I sat outside *a lot*. I felt truly happy. I wasn't constantly "stimulated" by all the commonplace interruptions of the world because life on the road in an RV means that you don't always have a good internet connection. At first, this inconvenience was a real nuisance. But it ended up being one of the best things that could have ever happened to me. Not being able to remain constantly connected helped me break the patterns of being so dependent on our gadgets and get away from the endless scrolling and checking of email folders.

My anxiety and depression were finally getting under control again. If you haven't discovered this for yourself yet, social media and over-working are HUGE contributors to anxiety and depression, especially for me. And for the first time, I even felt like COVID had leveled the playing field for all photographers simply because we ALL were affected, no matter how well-known or successful we were or had been. I no longer felt stuck in a house working 12 hours a day (or more) so I could keep up or surpass everyone else in order to feel worthy. No, life on the road was a good balance of work mixed with new experiences, spending time together, and some days just sitting in the sun.

And slowly, a little at a time, my photography business began coming back. New weddings were being scheduled. Yay! And re-bookings of postponed weddings were also finding their way to me, making the fall look promising for a change. I had also learned that I didn't need the big house and all the "other stuff" to be happy. For the first time ever, I decided that I could step back from shooting so much, live a simpler life, and we would be just fine. So, after a year of losing everything but finding peace again, the big house, the new expensive cars, and designer brands had lost their appeal.

I felt that I could finally breathe again, and I was just months away from turning 50! I was planning on celebrating it all month long! Heck, I had probably been planning my entire life because, in my house, birthdays are a BIG deal! And a person only turns 50 once.

In addition to weddings returning, photography workshops and in-person events were slowly making a comeback. Teaching for workshops is my jam and after almost a year of not being together and not shooting, photographers happily welcomed the chance to travel and be creative again. And since we were already in Florida, I launched three one-day workshops at a gorgeous venue in Miami and filled them up almost the moment I announced them. I was back! I was on that high again because teaching brings me so much joy.

Once you are a teacher, you are always a teacher; it never truly goes away. I finally felt like the sun was starting to shine again. The long winter was over and I was ready to soar.

The pandemic had taught me a lot, and although it a little worse for wear, my business was still standing. Believe it or not though, as crazy as it sounds, I was grateful for some of the changes that COVID had brought. I had realized that, depending on what you are talking about, "less *is* more," and money does not bring happiness. In fact, the only thing that I could readily perceive about money was that the more of it I had, the more it exposed how ridiculous my priorities can be, and *that* caused some REAL stress. I realized that my priorities either needed to shift or needed to be relocated altogether because family and peace became way more important than my career. Ahhhhh. I finally felt like I was coming into such a good place.

But can you sense another plot twist coming? The universe was preparing its next illusion, its next sleight-of-hand trick to make me recoil in despair. What do wise people say when life starts getting easy again? "Just wait. A ball is about to drop." For us, though, there were a number of balls ready to fall, and when they did drop, they almost crushed us in the process.

Because, almost exactly a year to the day of the pandemic being declared, just when we were starting to see the light at the end of our tunnel, we received some news that would emotionally devastate us, reshaping life as we knew it, then and for the future. And we would never ever be, or feel, the same in our world.

Up until now, it seemed like one "C" word—COVID—was enough. We had navigated our way through it as best we could and had emerged with only a few scrapes, scratches, and bruises. But the alphabet wasn't finished with us. "C" was not just for "cookie," and it certainly wasn't good enough for me. Or us.

My father-in-law had been experiencing some health issues, as one does. Personally, I was busy for the next two weeks traveling and teaching workshops. And now that they had been officially scheduled, I couldn't just drop them after waiting so long to have that part of my existence back. So, Matt and I decided that he and Mari-Kate would head up to Ohio to check in on his dad, and I would fly up there when I was finished. I mean, at the time, it didn't seem like anything was too serious regarding Dad's health. But, understandably, he could use some help with things around the house. And since our life was pretty flexible, it made sense for them to head up to Ohio. But, a week later we heard the word "cancer." Yes, another "C-word" that changed our life in an instant. Matt's dad had bladder cancer.

Up until now, no one in our family had gone through any major cancer requiring chemo. My mom and my sister each had melanoma but, after surgery, they were cancer-free. We soon found out that Dad was going to need both surgery *and* chemo. We also understood that it was likely going to be rough because of his age. He was already 82.

Matt and I decided that, for the time being, we would come off the road. We would move the RV to Ohio and live in it while we cared for Dad and Mom. I would fly when I needed to travel for business. The optimist in me would downplay the severity and tell me, "This is just a little hiccup. It will all be okay. Dad will get better. The world will get better. And we will get back to traveling and planning out the rest of our lives."

But that didn't happen.

Because the last week in May of 2021 would be the start of the hardest season of our life. It would completely shake me to my core and, I'm sad to admit this, even my faith in God would be questioned.

But, before I go there, we need to go back to 1986, big hair and all.

PART 1:
CHAPTER 2

HELLO REALITY

"Remember, things don't happen TO us,

they happen FOR us.

It's all about perspective."

Julie Paisley

1986

I guess you could call me pretty fortunate because I made it through 15 years of my life experiencing what many would call a "perfect life." You can call me naïve if you want, but for the record, I was well aware of how fortunate I was. Up until that point, I honestly do not even remember anything in my life being a real struggle, mentally or physically, and anything that was "challenging" was just something I needed to roll up my sleeves for so I didn't get dirty. Yep, I lived that fairytale life, and a "bad day" for me was when McDonald's left the pickles on my cheeseburger or if I was out of hairspray.

By high school, I had accepted and was living as if my life could never be simple or average. God had gifted me with certain talents, and it was time to step into my greatness and change the world. Life had become my stage, and I had convinced myself that I was a super-heroine just like my alter ego, Anne of Green Gables. All I really needed now was the right cape to match the outfit with the rolled-up sleeves, as well as the rest of my self-glorified persona.

I had learned how to not be that shy little girl anymore. And since I had dismissed that person long ago, only one of two things could be true. Either I was meant to do great things, or my life would be dreadfully tragic. And since I was not open to the latter, I was determined that people would one day know who I was. I was groomed for this. I had done my best to forget all about that shy little girl because there was no way *she* would ever be good enough to do great things. I had turned into this person who ultimately held herself to such a high standard that I was convinced I had to be the best in order to prove my worth. I couldn't lose because I wasn't allowed to. I needed to be smart. I needed to use all my talents. I needed to be pretty, funny, and popular because all those things needed to be *factual* in order for me to be liked.

By the age of 15, I had developed a very unhealthy drive to achieve, and it far surpassed what a normal 15-year-old should ever feel. Now, anyone can argue that "A Drive to Achieve" is not necessarily a bad thing. And that, by itself anyway, is 100% true.

But let's consider, just for a moment, that because the name of this chapter is "Hello Reality," I feel it necessary to present you with two thoughts:

- There is a personality behind the person.
- There is a person behind the personality.

These two thoughts look so similar, but they have enormously different meanings. So, go ahead and ask yourself which one is deeper or more fundamental? And which one is more *you*?

You can almost answer these questions by asking another one: what time of day, or season, or life, are we talking about? But let's go a step further as well, because when that drive to achieve becomes *The Person* or *The Personality* behind the other, you realize you are looking through different ends of the same lens. And when *that* happens, you have to consider one additional question: what is the impact on the self? I was about to find out whether I wanted to or not.

But let's get back to me at the age of 15, because in the back of my mind, there were these strange, nagging questions that only came to me when I *wasn't* looking in the mirror. For example, I could be walking to class after lunch and, out of the blue, these thoughts hit me. The thoughts would ask, *"To whom am I actually trying to prove my worth? Who is that person in the mirror that never speaks up for herself?"* And, *"Shouldn't I at least try to get to know her?"*

I ignored those questions. I had become a machine of a person who was super-driven and motivated to make a difference. This super-hyper-overdrive and motivation would propel me further in a few years, as I would end up being the first one in my entire family to go to college. I didn't know it yet, but I would be the one to leave my small town and travel the world. What I did know was that I would become famous in my own right, somehow, someway, someday. I would not be constrained. I was going to take this drive and motivation and let it carry me to the next level. No matter the cost.

That is, until the day my body failed me. And in doing so it said, "Hello reality."

One minute I was a 15-year-old girl who had dreams of getting my driver's license, having a boyfriend, hanging out with my friends, going to college, and accomplishing everything my horizon could handle. Heck, I even knew that I wanted to be a broadcaster on TV. Woohoo! *The Today Show*, here I come!

But no, I was now a damaged girl. I couldn't even take a bath without my mom sitting on the other side of the shower curtain because of the possibility that I could suddenly have a seizure and drown. Yeah . . . hello reality. Thank you ever-so-much.

To be honest, I don't even remember a single thing from the first time it happened. Really. Not even a microsecond. Maybe it caused so much trauma that I permanently blocked it from my memory. What I do know from the aftermath of the event is that I had good people around me who made all the difference.

In any case, that first episode is still a mystery to me. Very much like I became a mystery to all the doctors trying to understand my condition. You see, seizures usually have a pattern, but mine did not. I had all the different types of seizures from grand mal to petit mal, as well as everything in between and off to the side. My life, and the lives of everyone around me, suddenly changed and I was facing a catalog of new norms. These included hospital visits and specialists, CAT scans and MRIs, EEGs and IVs. And on top of all that, someone was always assigned to be with me. I wasn't allowed to be left alone. I couldn't drive. Even my friends had to become familiar with, *and know*, the drill: insert the bite stick and protect my head and my body from being hurt in a fall or during convulsions. And then, of course, they would need to dry my tears when I eventually came out of it, all embarrassed and thoroughly scared.

And this was how I got my new nickname. I was now openly called "Flounder" to my face and it seemed fitting due to the situation I found myself in. I mean, the reference was obvious enough, but it was far from flattering. A flounder, after it's caught, lies on its back and flops around all over the place. Fitting, huh? Everyone thought it was cute, except me, of course. Thus began a new angle in my years of people-pleasing. I wouldn't speak up and say that it hurt me. Nope. I would laugh along with them all. Because as long as I went along with them, it made them happy. And if they were happy, they would like me.

I don't even remember my 10th grade year. Or more accurately, I have this collection of fragments in my mind that I could probably try to arrange in some kind of mosaic, but I don't know where to even begin because they are all mixed around like the ingredients of a pot of stew. Anyway, most of my 10th grade year was spent sleeping because the seizures would just exhaust me. Plus, all the medications turned me into a zombie. My "perfect" family started suffering because everyone and everything else was put on the back burner. It was suddenly all about me. And the worst thing about it was that I felt that it was all my fault. I believed I had done something wrong to cause this terrible thing that was happening to me and affecting my family.

Before I move on, I'm going to take a timeout for a minute to talk about something that is super hard for me to say out loud, much less write about it in a book for all the world to see. And before I say this, I want you to know that *I am* a believer and I love Jesus with all of my heart. My faith means everything to me and I know that I would be nothing without God in my life.

I also want you to know that I don't blame my parents, or even the leaders in my church, for what I am about to say. I truly believe that they did not know better. This is what they were taught to believe. It's a vicious cycle of misinterpretation of the Bible from man's perspective, and it's so harmful but, again, I do not cast the blame on anyone. But this is a vital part of my story, and it needs to be said.

So here it goes.

As an adult, I have realized that the church, as well as organized religion in general, can cause deep religious trauma. It's taken me a long time of soul-searching, studying, and forgiveness to get to where I am now. And only after this searching have I been able to see God as loving and forgiving, and NOT just a God of wrath. I see now that I feared God in a very unhealthy way. I didn't see Him as loving and kind. I was literally terrified of Him. And honestly, my drive to be "good" was out of fear and not really because it was a conviction I would die for.

In my church, I was taught to believe that if anything bad happens in your life, it's because of your sin and this is just how God delivers His punishment. But I realized this was just plain *harmful*. Viewing God this way and thinking of Him in this manner is really screwed up. I do believe that sometimes God uses circumstances to get our attention, but that's not always the case and it's definitely not to punish us. I was not having seizures because I was living in sin—I was 15 years old! And I was a GOOD girl. Sure, I told a lie here and there, and I could certainly have an attitude if I wanted. But waking up one day and being suddenly afflicted with a dangerous and life-threatening illness was not caused because of some great sin.

The worst things I had ever done were almost laughable. I would occasionally listen to the *Delilah at Night* radio show with all that "ungodly" music. One time, I took a piece of hay from the town nativity scene during a scavenger hunt. And another time, I rolled my eyes at my mom. Wow! I was such a rebel.

But seriously, I wasn't some stupid, poorly raised 15-year-old girl sneaking out of the house at night to cause mischief. Heck no. In fact, I had never even kissed a boy before. But now, I was being asked by elders and pastors in my church if I was having sex because, to them, it would "make sense" that my sickness was a result of a hidden sin. I was even told at one point that I had a demon and they needed to anoint me with oil and to lay hands on me to get the demon out. Now this was seriously messed up! I mean, what level of cruelty is required to tell a scared teenage girl that because her body is sick, she has a demon living inside her? Did they think I had met this demon on the way home from school and invited him in? "Hey, come play inside my body for a while, it will be fun. I'm having dinner around 7:00 so we have a few hours."

Yeah, so like I said—that is seriously messed up. It's so messed up, in fact, that I can totally understand why people might be afraid of joining a church in the first place.

And I'm sure that there are those of you reading this right now who do believe that God is all about wrath and judgment. But honestly, believing in God *in that way* is wrong. Plain and simple. And, as what happened in my case, if someone thinks they need to force this "wrath and judgment" on a confused, scared, and worried teenager in order to make her think that, because she made a mistake, God, Himself, afflicted her with demonic possession . . . well, that comes under the heading of *inexcusable.*

So go ahead and disagree with me on this if you want. But in my eyes, it's not up for debate because I remember going to the altar and praying fervently that God would reveal my sin to me so I could ask His forgiveness and be healed. But at 15 years old, when there was no immediate response, I started believing the new-and-improved lie that something *was* wrong with me and that I *deserved* to be punished. And this, in turn, proved to me that I had been right along. I was never good enough just being *me.*

So, what the heck was I gonna do now? I would have to "unbecome" me. Julie was not good enough. Julie was flawed. Julie would never amount to anything. Jesus did not love Julie the way she was, so I had to *do* more and *be* more. I even set up a list of preliminary rules for myself:

- This new Julie needed to be extraordinary.
- She needed to be bigger than life.
- She will not settle for anything less than the best.
- Being broken is not acceptable.

It is worth noting that I recognize how naïve and youthful this silly little list actually is. But this list, all by itself, with all of its under-developed limitations, really shaped my conviction of what I believed my worth was based on. I came to believe that I had no worth at all unless I was actively pursuing and cognitively attaining that high standard. **All. The. Time.** It was only *then* that I could *begin* to be worthy.

In my own eyes, I had *no choice* other than to be perfect. I had to succeed at everything because I convinced myself that being perfect meant that I would truly be loved. I had to withdraw and revoke any *feelings* that I felt about myself. I mean, *what good are feelings, anyway?* Well, there may be millions of answers, but I'm just not going there right now.

I couldn't be shy or "normal." Not me. I had to be special and I had to over-achieve. And *that* was the "hard shell" to everything about me. Yes, I knew I needed to appear tough and that I needed to be strong. So, I grew this "shell," this protective overcoat that allowed me to hide the other weaknesses.

But most importantly, and pardon me while I wipe the tears out of my glasses, underneath that shell, what I really needed to know was that God would love and accept me. And if He did, *I would no longer be broken.* And *that* was worth striving for! Oh, how I wish I could go back to that 15-year-old girl and tell her that God loves and uses broken vessels all the time, and that she was already perfect in His sight.

Fortunately, and speaking as an adult again, I was able to brush away just enough of the confusion to realize that I truly LOVED God and would strive to serve Him each and every day. But when we let man interpret the Bible on his own with imperfect terms, things get really messed up. After all, man is only human. We are only *in the image* of God, and therefore limited. By extension, man simply does not, and cannot, know everything. As a result, all of our efforts will be, at best, either slightly misguided, or perhaps a little short of the goals God has for us. It pains me to think how many souls never come to know Jesus because of this. Surely, the world would be a better place if more people accepted that Jesus corrects that misguidance and makes God's goals for us both accessible and tangible.

Anyway, about a year after the seizures started, they were finally under control. As long as I took my medicine and kept my sugar regulated, I would go weeks and sometimes months without having one. Slowly, my independence was coming back. I still couldn't drive a car, but my friends were more than willing to take me anywhere I wanted to go. I had a boyfriend. My parents were supportive of me in all issues. My grades were great. I was captain of the cheerleading squad. I was popular and pretty. I could sing. I could act. I could write. I won awards. I had already been accepted into the college of my choice. I had finally made it, and because I was so good, my perfect life was back.

At least, that is what I tried to tell myself. Because on a daily basis, I still lived with negative thoughts about myself. And no matter how hard I tried and prayed, I was never enough.

If you asked anyone who knew me, I'm sure they would say that I seemed so confident. I never met a stranger that I didn't instantly make friends with. Any goal that I put out in front of me, I aced it. Yep. I had conquered high school with flying colors. Bring on college! I was ready for it. But again, hello reality. I was in for a rude awakening.

Try to imagine this: I was a girl who had never known life beyond home, church, and a school that I had attended my entire life with, quite literally, the very same people I had known since birth. And then, this same girl walks onto the campus of a private Christian college six hours away from home with 5,000 other students, not knowing a single other soul who attended. And here's where you get to criticize me for being sheltered and naïve. I walked on to that college campus, and suddenly that shy little 9-year-old girl was back. I was no longer the big fish in a small pond. Nobody knew who I was and no one cared about my accomplishments from high school. All my insecurities and fears came rushing back. I became homesick immediately and the onset of severe anxiety of "not being good enough," coupled with a fear of failure, became debilitating. I had never felt so small and unworthy in my entire life. Ben and Jerry became my best friends. Not the people, but the ice cream.

During my first semester, I struggled with my classes because I had never been in a traditional school setting where I had to listen to the teacher, take notes, and learn. In the private school that I had attended, we worked at our own pace with hands-on attention. It was *very* different from this new thing I found myself in called college.

I tried out for a singing group and, for the first time in my entire life, I didn't make the callbacks. So of course, to me, this meant that I was the ultimate failure. I once again fed myself the lie that just being me was not enough, and if I wanted to make something of myself, I had to change because failure was NOT an option and neither was mediocrity. Nope, I had to be the best or nothing at all. I was NOT made to blend in because that was never enough. It was time to become Super Julie. I did it in high school and I could do it again in college, no matter the stakes.

Now, I could elaborate on all the little things that made my arrival at college a wild and crazy roller coaster ride, but let's suffice to say that I somehow survived that very awkward first semester and had a little plan of sorts. I came back in the second semester with a vengeance. I decided that one major wasn't enough. I needed *two*. I tried out for another singing group and I made it. I also tried out for a musical and I made that too. I stressed over perfect grades and my little plan was proving to be a complete success. I had made myself so busy that I had no time to contemplate any type of imperfection in my life. I was well-liked by my teachers and peers because I knew how to perform, and I was unusually good at it. But there's more to the story.

Because at age 18, I started sacrificing my health in order to be the best. I didn't sleep. I didn't eat well. And yes, I gained the Freshman-15, but I wasn't done there. Not even close! That was way too easy. I was Super Julie, the overachiever, so I gained the Freshman-50.

My mom freaked out.

And so, my first summer home from college was spent going to the doctor to find out, once again, "What is wrong with Julie?" And by the end of the summer, we knew.

It turned out that at 19 years old, I had severe endometriosis and PCOS. And on top of that, the seizures had returned in full force due to a lack of sleep, self-imposed stress, and not eating properly. Which, when combined together in non-medical terms meant, "Hello future husband, not only can your wife stop, drop, and plop at any given moment, she also will more than likely never give you children."

Hello new reality. Hello rekindled trauma. Hello reminder that I'm not perfect and this sickness was again all my fault. Hello to me begging God, once again, to please reveal my sin so I could confess and wouldn't be punished further.

Because, since the age of 15, I truly believed that when bad things happened to me, it was because of me and my sin. So, surely, I had done something wrong and I deserved it. Right?

It's crazy how we train our minds and bodies to become something that we are not. And if you know me, I bet you have a hard time believing that deep down, in this over-the-top personality, this bubbly life of the party, the one that everyone wants to be around and is all about unicorns and rainbows and pink and sparkles online, is really that shy little 9-year-old girl who would be happy to spend the rest of her days in the English countryside. Because the truth is that the real me doesn't need designer brands and would rather dress like Anne of Green Gables and have sheep, a few goats, and a flower garden. I'm not sure if the real me even likes pink as much as I've led everyone to believe. Also, the real me doesn't need fifty thousand followers and if Instagram erased it all, I really wouldn't be upset in the slightest.

And yes, I know that it has taken me *years* to get here, but I honestly wouldn't mind a restart. I would almost rather just disappear out of the spotlight and into thin air because I'm not the Julie Paisley I was before 2020. I do think that If I could find a way to run my business without social media, I would do it in a heartbeat because I no longer need outward validation to feel valuable.

Why did I always believe that the real me wasn't enough? Why did I always feel like I needed to put on a show and be someone else that I dreamed up in my head in order to be liked?

I'm sure that many of you can relate to this very situation and that I'm not alone. Especially with the world of social media breathing down our necks all the time. Thank goodness that I didn't have to grow up with it. Just having to deal with it in my adult life has certainly been enough for me, if not too much. I remember my days as a teenager when getting a Walkman was a big deal. Oh, to go back to that period of time would be a nice change of scenery—a welcomed one. Life was a lot less complicated back then. Even though life was less complicated back in 1990, I hadn't yet gone through the hard life lessons that have brought me to the place of healing that I experience today.

But looking back, through the lens of time, I can see that I had once again convinced myself that I needed to be Super Julie. And Super Julie always ended up being what everyone expected. She dug deep and found that bigger than life personality. She was the good girl, the overachiever, the always popular, the one always striving to be the best and do more.

And yes, I know that for the sake of storytelling, I am laying all of this on pretty thick. I know it sounds like I was a shallow, even horribly conceited, person that was motivated only by praise and achievements. But deep down, if you *really* knew me, it wasn't me at all. I simply *became* that person because *shy Julie* wasn't enough. She was flawed. She was sick, and, in my mind, she would never be good enough to make it. Super Julie was where it was at because everyone loved her.

So, which question was more correct? Was I living the life of the personality behind the person or the person behind the personality? I certainly could not have answered that question then.

But being super, by definition, is not normal for anyone. And, this is not an exaggeration, I could have easily died during my junior year of college. It was easily the hardest year I had during college. I was taking 19 hours of classes per week in a Performance and Education double major and I was running on empty with only four hours of sleep each night. Also, I had taken on other exhausting extracurricular leadership roles. And even communicating it all to you here, I can feel myself getting tired just trying to explain it. So, I'm just going to cut to the chase and state plainly that all the extra hours I forced on myself, whether in special singing groups or musical productions or whatever, had finally gotten the best of me.

And WHAM! I suddenly became *very* ill. I had become so ill, in fact, that my school made a special exception for me and sent me home for a week to recover. Generally speaking, colleges NEVER do this. A small town private high school might care enough to do this, but college? It's unheard of. And for a while, to be honest, I wasn't even sure that I would ever return. I had, once again, worn my body down in my striving to be the best in order to feel worthy. If only that 20-year-old me would have learned her lesson back then.

I'm sure by now you have a reasonable understanding of who I was at the time—or at least who I thought I should be. You are probably thinking, "Enough already! Let's move on, Julie! This self-inflicted harm is getting old." But unfortunately, it was just the beginning of many years of abusing my body and sacrificing my health to be everything for everyone else. I had created a monster. And that monster would not be fully released for another 30 years.

On the brighter side of things, though, I did make it through college. And I made it through alive, which was more or less beneficial. I graduated with honors, and was only one class away from having a perfect 4.0 grade point average my senior year. And while I could have chosen to be bitter over that one stupid class where I received a B+, in the grand scheme of life, not graduating with a perfect 4.0 didn't really bother me.

Besides, I now knew what it meant to be an adult, and during my senior year, I started dating one of my best friends. I had found some real personal joy—some actual happiness that wasn't self-imposed. I went on to graduate. We got engaged. Got married. And we landed our dream jobs which were offered through the college. We were chosen to travel throughout the United States, visiting schools and churches everywhere, in order to tell them about our wonderful little college in the deep south.

And like all the years past, life was good until it wasn't.

PART 1:
CHAPTER 3

ROCK-A-BYE BABY

"I was created for this difficult yet beautiful experience and my joy would come in His time."

Julie Paisley

1993

We kinda broke the rules. With our new job, we were not supposed to get pregnant for at least two years due to the requirements of us being on the road 11 months of the year. But, I had already been told by several medical professionals that getting pregnant would be super challenging. To myself, I secretly hoped that it *would* happen, so we were not really trying to be careful. Of course, and somewhat as expected, no baby came. And while that may have been easier for my foreseeable work life, it really started another cascade of trauma in realizing, every month, that I was once again flawed.

Nope. I hadn't learned my lesson and I was not even good enough to bring a child into the world. It was a silent battle that I faced. It was in the early 90s and people just didn't talk about infertility like they do now. Nowadays, it seems like some people proudly wear their infirmities on their sleeves. Back then, you might write about it in your diary. Whereas today, some people post it on social media and start a Go-Fund-Me.

Anyway, my husband wasn't fazed by it. He wanted children but was not in a big hurry. But for me, this was like a dagger to my heart. C'mon, getting pregnant is a normal thing and it's what our bodies were made for. People do it every day. It's part of God's divine plan. We are commanded to be fruitful and multiply. Well, it appeared that it didn't apply to me.

Hello trauma, my old friend. Why is this happening to me? What hidden sin is in my life again?

I didn't know it at the time, but this was when depression and high-functioning anxiety really started for me. I experienced a little during college, but it became intense in the first few years of our marriage. It went untreated for years and years because, again, if you have mental illness or depression, it's because you don't trust God enough and nobody talks about that.

Nope. You don't talk about mental illness in a Baptist church because mental illness is a sin problem. Find the sin, confess it, trust God more, and you will be okay. But I was not okay and I wouldn't be for a very long time.

During the second year of our marriage, I ended up in emergency surgery in Ohio. We were on the road at that time, traveling for our job with our alma mater, but we made it to the town my in-laws were in. I will never forget having to sign a paper at 23 years old to give them permission to do a hysterectomy if, after they opened me up, they found it to be necessary. I can still remember that moment so vividly and I truly thought my life was over. But the good news was, my life did not end and I did not have to have a hysterectomy at the age of 23.

However, I was once again reminded that my chances of having a baby were very slim. And with that came the bottled-up anxieties from so many years ago that I was broken and so full of sin that of course I was being punished. So, I begged God to please fix me. To please show me how to change myself in order to reveal the deeply hidden sin in my life that kept punishing me. I felt He hated me and slowly I started hating Him as well.

But I had become so good at controlling my feelings on the outside, there was no way I was ever going to let anybody see that. In some ways, I literally thought I was the perfect Christian. I graduated from a Christian college, worked for that same Christian college, and now I was out in the real world teaching at a Christian school. I sang in the choir and I participated in special music programs at church every week. They don't let just anyone take on these roles, right? I was devoted to the church and my life seemed to completely revolve around it.

But my heart became harder and my resentment grew right on schedule every month.

For six years, I suffered through infertility. I put my body through surgeries, medications, and monthly shots. We experienced losses and disappointments. I gained 80 pounds. Yes, you read that correctly. Eighty pounds! I didn't even know who I was anymore and I masked it all with a smile and a laugh because that's what good Christians do.

1998

I will never forget the last time IVF failed. I knew it was over. My body had gone through so much that now I was having cardiac and vision issues. My anxiety and depression were beyond what a normal person should handle. I thought I was coming apart at the seams and I was darn-near killing myself to have a child. And then my husband held my face in his hands and said, "Julie, this is enough. It's not worth losing you to have a child."

And for me, that was it.

BOOM.

I had become the ultimate failure and was past the point of no return. Women were made to give birth. But no, not me. Talk about a slap in the face. Had I lost so much favor in the eyes of God that I was not even good enough to do what our bodies are made to do? And then to make it unbearably worse, my younger sister, who had only been married a few months and wasn't even trying to have a baby, had learned that she was pregnant.

My mom was the one who ended up giving me the news. I remember screaming and falling to my knees in tears from the overwhelming pain because I was just so angry at God. I had devoted so much of my life to Him and this is how He thanks me? I had done everything right and I was a GOOD person by all standards. I lived a good Christian life. I dedicated my life to ministry, but at that moment, the emotional pain was so intense that it had become physical pain. And if you have never experienced it, that's what heartache actually is. It felt so real and so deep in every fiber of my being, I don't know how I remember anything from that moment. Even now, as I'm writing this today, tears are streaming down my face, fogging my glasses, and I feel my heart being ripped from my body almost like it's happening all over again. That day, at that very moment, until November of 2021, was the worst experience of my life.

After a short time, when I had regained muscular and skeletal control of my body, I remember jumping in the car and taking off. I had no idea where I was going. I just drove because nothing made sense. Tears were streaming down my face and I kept screaming at God. I literally hated Him at that moment. I wanted to die. I didn't care about anything or anyone anymore. Nothing mattered. If you've seen the movie *Brave*, you probably remember the scene when Merida jumps on her horse and flees at full speed through the forest. That was me at the wheel of a car, pushing the equivalent of two hundred horses down the road. It's a wonder that I made it back home in one piece.

I'm probably going to say something right now that goes against all religious teaching, but it is okay if you feel this way about God right now. Because, at that moment, as well as several other moments in my life after that, I was angry at God. "Hate" is a strong word, but I have, in fact, felt hate for Him at times when I didn't view Him as loving at all. I viewed Him as a monster—a figure who had all the authority to make your life a living hell. I viewed Him as a punisher. I viewed Him as unmerciful and that He never truly cared about me.

And in some sick way, I imagined that He actually enjoyed me thinking in this way.

But oh, my friend, I'm here to say that the way I see God now is so different. I now firmly believe that on that day, He was crying along with me the whole time. He felt my pain, and if I would have let Him, He would have wrapped His loving arms around me and held me as I wept. On this side of heaven, we will never understand why bad things are allowed to happen. And I've learned that it's not ours to understand. We never will while we're in this place. But I also feel strongly now that all of the difficulty I experienced was *because* I was deeply loved by God. It wasn't punishment. No, it was the opposite, He had created me perfectly in His sight and He wept with me as I was going through all this pain. He knew how these things needed to happen in my life in order for me to help others in the future. I was created for this difficult yet beautiful experience and my joy would come in His time.

In some ways, I feel like I have the nine lives of a cat. There have been three times in my life where I wanted to take my own life, but God prevented that from happening. This was the first. I secretly hoped for a car crash so I could die. And as I was driving, I can't even tell you how often I wanted to run through a red light, drive straight into oncoming traffic, or just drive right off a bridge. I even felt like I may have run right over a few of my angels that day.

Hours later, I finally stopped driving. All my tears were gone. I felt as if they dried up in the wind just so they could fall on me again someday. I don't know if you have ever physically been to the point where you can no longer cry but it's a horrible feeling. In a way, I had just had my "Jacob moment." I had wrestled with God, but He won. Little did I know, however, that my miracle would be coming soon. In fact, she was already in her birth mother's belly on the other side of the world. How ironic, huh?

The days, weeks, and months following my wrestling match with God were nothing but a blur. I was in such a haze of depression and anxiety that I went on autopilot. There was very little substance in those nine months that I remember, until my nephew was born in August. I remember being the first one to hold him, and I just looked at him, sobbing. That is something that I remember extremely well.

In one respect, it was the happiest day because he was here and he was healthy. But for me, it was also the saddest day in the sense that I was mourning that this experience might never happen for me.

But I guess God has a sense of humor because I'm almost four years older than my sister. I was supposed to deliver my parents' first grandchild. I mean, it's logical, right? I was married first, so it was only fair! And guess what? On the other side of the world, a baby girl was born a month premature in a little village in Russia. Her birth mother could not care for her and she was left at the hospital with a letter and the hopes of adoption in her immediate future. This little baby girl would become my daughter. She was born in July. And Dylan, my nephew, was born in August. So yes, I do have the oldest grandchild. God is funny like that. He loves us so much that

He gives us little winks to let us know how much He really cares.

And just like in scripture, as Jacob had been wounded from wrestling with God, I was also left wounded after my bout. But slowly, my faith started to come back. Even as I am writing this chapter, I'm healing and realizing that I still need to release some of the anguish from those years of my life.

As a woman, not being able to carry and birth a child, as we had been designed to do, makes you feel like you are not normal. You feel like you are a broken vessel. Like you were deprived of the very purpose that you were put on this earth for. It is a pain like no other.

If you are reading this book and going through my same struggle, I want you to wrap your arms around yourself and feel a hug from me. I told you that I was a hugger, and I'm even good at it remotely. But I want you to know, *truly know*, that there is NOTHING WRONG WITH YOU. You are worthy, you are complete, your story is just not finished yet.

Slowly, I started coming back to grips with day-to-day life. During this time, I just focused on my work. I was a Kindergarten teacher, a music teacher, a drama teacher, and a cheerleading coach. Since I didn't have children of my own, I poured everything I possibly could into everyone else's children. And quite literally, being a teacher was the best thing in the world for me at that time. It was helping me to heal and it temporarily filled the void that had been so prevalent in my life.

So naturally, given my situation, I wanted to adopt a child. I just wanted to be a mom. And at that point, becoming a mom by adoption was okay with me. Matt, however, wasn't quite ready for it yet. We had talked about it, but due to the fact that six years of infertility treatments had basically broken us financially, it just seemed like it would never happen for us. I had accepted the fact that I may never have children, and for some reason, this must be what God had planned for me. That is, until the day I had an event that was random to me, but clearly not too random to God.

On this day, in February of 1999, we had a yard sale.

Did you ever realize that God can show His presence amongst the things that we no longer see as having any real value? Now, I'm going to need to pause for a moment because just as I wrote the above sentence, I had a Jesus-moment.

You see, during a yard sale we get rid of things we no longer see as valuable. However, to the person who comes to see what is being offered, our cast-offs take on a new value, uniquely intrinsic to both the shopper and the items themselves. I had personally felt like I was one of God's cast-offs and that I was no longer valuable to Him. *But I was so unbelievably wrong.* Oh, how ironic it is that God used that random yard sale to introduce me to the person who would help us bring home our daughter! And if you don't have goosebumps right now, you need to get that fixed.

For some reason, among other items, I was selling a map at my yard sale. It was one that I had used in my teaching over time, and it was sitting out on the table next to me. I still can see and hear this conversation as clear as day. Two ladies walked over the table with the map. The one with the dark hair said to the other, "A map, I wonder if it's on here." She took a moment to look carefully and then pointed out a place on the map. "Ahh! Yes, it's here! I have to buy this to show the boys," she said.

I was suddenly a little nosy, which is totally not like me, and asked her if she was going on a trip. She smiled big and said, "Yes, we are heading to this part of Russia to pick up our daughter next month." I said, "Wow! Are you adopting?" And she answered, "Yes." At that moment, I had never felt a more divine intervention in my life. I got goosebumps as I asked her to tell me more about it, and before she left, I had the number for an international adoption agency. And somehow, deep in my bones, I *knew* without a shadow of a doubt that my daughter was in Russia and we would be bringing her home soon. Now I just needed to break the news to my husband.

Now, here's something you need to know about my husband and me. I'm spontaneous. *Matt is not.* He's a facts guy. He needs all the information upfront. And then he needs *weeks* to think about it. But if something feels right to me, I'm all in. Even if it seems impossible. Because somehow, someway, sooner rather than later, I'm going to make it happen. We could not be more opposite.

I stared at that number on the piece of paper and I called. Within an hour, I knew all the prices and all the details. I had more information than my husband was ready to handle and I had the conviction to press forward to make it happen. International adoption from Russia had just recently opened up to the world. It was still a newly recognized option and there were lots of people who were skeptical about the authenticity of the program. But as the yard sale lady could prove to me herself, it was *real*. And it was fast. It was a done deal. No birth mother would change her mind. Those children were in orphanages and needed homes. As long as you could come up with 40K, the baby was yours.

Keep in mind that this was back in 1999. 40K was the price of a small house in my area and we were just about flat-broke. We were also up to our ears in debt. With our salaries combined, we brought home about $500 a week as teachers. There was NO WAY we could afford this, but I KNEW it was going to happen. I knew in my heart that our daughter was there waiting for us.

Now you may want to blink a few times here because I called Matt, rushed through the story of how I met this woman at the yard sale, and how she gave me this number which I called right away, and they told me it would cost this much and that they actually had a baby girl who was available right now who had special needs and had been turned down by two families already, and the lady at the agency was faxing her picture over to us at his work right now and I'm jumping in the car and coming to his office, okay, bye!

That was the ecstatically overjoyed conversation I had with him. I don't think I let him say even one complete word through the call, maybe just a few syllables if he was lucky. And a few minutes later, a faxed picture of a tiny 7-month old baby girl came through at his work. A coworker asked who it was, and he said, "It's my daughter." Yes! Either he was already on board or he simply knew there was no way to change my mind.

This was February of 1999. And a few months later, in June, two scared 28-year-olds boarded a plane to Russia with $20K in cash on each of their bodies, all in twenty-dollar bills.

Have you ever seen $20K in only twenty-dollar denominations? It's really bulky. It's a lot of money for two people to be carrying strapped to their bodies and hidden in their clothes while entering a foreign country. Especially when that country was *Russia*. It was the most terrifying moment in my life. But love makes you do crazy things and I will never ever forget that trip for the rest of all eternity.

I remember watching the movie *Groundhog Day* over and over again on the plane. I remember being so tired. I remember going through customs being afraid that they would find all the money on us and take us to jail. I remember walking out of the airport, fearing that we were going to be robbed and left for dead. I remember hearing our names being called and running into the arms of friends from college who were also there adopting at the same time and we had no idea about the others' plans. I remember thinking, "Is this another wink from God?"

I remember our interpreter showing us around Moscow. I remember the scariest plane ride of my life, in which our luggage was loaded on to the plane from the back of a beat-up pickup truck. I remember the plane looking like there was no way it would get in the air without falling apart. I remember thinking it looked so bad that I was pretty sure there was duct tape involved.

I remember chickens being on the plane, in the cabin with the actual human livestock. I remember the smell—oh my goodness, the smell! No air conditioning and no deodorant. Just a plane full of sweaty bodies and an unknowable number of chickens. For the first time ever, I had to use a barf bag on the plane. Sorry for that visual.

I remember landing in what looked like a war zone. I remember the cries of the children in the orphanage. I remember our daughter being brought down the stairs to us and how she wouldn't stop staring at me and how I couldn't stop crying. I remember having to leave her at the orphanage three days in a row and only getting to spend a few hours with her each day. I remember standing in that Russian court and being made her legal parents. I remember the plane ride home where she cried and cried because she wasn't used to being held.

But, through all of that, what I remember most was the joy of knowing that I was finally a mom. And maybe God did love me after all.

PART 1:
CHAPTER 4

THEY CALL ME MOMMY

"She was my reason for living.
She was the reason that I was put on this
earth. And for the first time in my life,
I felt complete and whole."

Julie Paisley

Something magical happens when you become a mom. Suddenly the only thing that matters in the world is this new little person that has come into your life. You no longer buy things for you and you realize it's okay to look homeless as long as your child is wearing the cutest matching clothes from head to toe. And of course, your one-year-old needs the right shoes and a color-coordinated bow to match for every single outfit. One of the most fun parts for any mom is that your baby girl needs multiple changes of clothes throughout the day. This way, you can continually take her picture because, you know, the last time you took her picture was already twenty minutes ago.

Oh, and the toys! She has to have them all, right? *She is your life.* You read and play with her all day long while your husband brings home takeout for the fourth time this week because you couldn't leave her sweet little face long enough to cook.

I became consumed with this tiny little person. She was my reason for living. She was the reason that I was put on this earth. And for the first time in my life, I felt complete and whole. I didn't feel like I needed to put on a show and become someone else in order to be enough. I was enough for her and that was all that mattered.

Life was so good. We had a humble but beautiful home that we owned. My husband had a new fancy job and was making enough money, so I didn't really have to work. I had fulfilled my dream of being a stay-at-home mom with Mari-Kate, but was still able to teach music part-time at the school and bring her with me.

She was the cutest. She had the best personality and giggle in the world. Everyone adored her. We knew she had special needs, but we just thought that through therapy and early intervention she would be okay. She was diagnosed with fetal alcohol syndrome (which was super common in children adopted from Russia) and failure to thrive, but I'm a fixer and I just knew with enough love and education, she would be okay. But a few years later, we were told that she had autism. I didn't think it would affect me but it did.

All of the sudden, the progression of her life was changed, but the funny thing is, it didn't bother her or her dad. Or my parents. Or anyone around us. No. It bothered *me*. I suddenly started mourning the "normal" life that would never be hers. And then my past came back and the lies that I had believed, but had hidden away, became real again. I was once again being punished. God hated me. I was living in unconfessed sin.

Looking back, I see now that I was making it all about me. It was time for another pity-party about how God hated me so much and I was so blinded and full of myself that I didn't notice how dangerous the path I was walking on actually was. So, before I continue any further, I want to stop here for a minute and address that "woe is me syndrome." It's very dangerous, my friend. It's quite common when someone goes through a lot in their life and suffers through trauma to start looking at everything that is happening TO THEM and not FOR THEM.

Resentment and comparison start settling in. You start telling God it's not fair. You play the victim. That you don't deserve this. You become bitter and manipulating. You become selfish and make everything about you. And you have no idea it's happening, but everyone else does. This was me. But I will come back to this later.

Mari-Kate turned two and I was ready for another baby. And by this point, my body had been healing for several years and my doctors thought if we tried IVF one more time, it just might work. And to make it better, insurance would pay for it. And *that* was the icing on the cake!

So I made the appointment.

The Friday before my appointment, the nurse called to ask me some questions. The first one she asked was when my last period was. I couldn't remember. It was somewhat normal for me to miss periods. My body was so messed up from all the years of infertility treatments, as well as the endometriosis, I honestly wasn't all that keen on keeping track anymore.

But no. This date was important for us to proceed with the treatments. I tried to think back, but we had just gone through a very traumatic experience with my sister. She had almost died after giving birth to her second child, and now I was being grilled because I didn't keep track of my cycle. Ha, that's a good one.

The nurse told me I had to do a pregnancy test before I came in. I rolled my eyes. Seriously! Didn't she realize the trauma that these tests put me through? I was kinda angry if you really want to know how I felt. But I had been given clinical instructions, so I went to the store to satisfy the conditions of the task, rolling my eyes at least a couple more times on the way there, and one more time when I took the box off the shelf. I had told Matt that we needed milk. So, I bought the milk that I head faked Matt with, as well as a 2-pack pregnancy test while I just continued to grumble about having to do another one of these things. I don't think I have ever been so annoyed with having to take a pregnancy test. Honestly, if you could see the thoughts in my head, you would think that I was going in for a beating or something equally intimidating. It's only a *test*, Julie. Just pee on the stick and confirm what you already know—that there is no way you are pregnant without medical intervention. I knew the drill.

But within seconds, I saw something on that test that I had never seen before. It said *pregnant*.

Pregnant? NO WAY.

No lie. No joke. No exaggeration. As soon as that test showed positive, I immediately had to throw up. I just laid there on the bathroom floor for a while because I was in shock. It had to be wrong, right? We had been married for almost eight years and there was NO WAY we got pregnant on our own. I drank a lot of water. I did the second test and poof—again, positive.

Friend, this was a day that I had dreamed about *for a very long time*. I had been pregnant twice before but didn't even know it until I miscarried. Eight years of trying to get pregnant, with six of those years going through intense infertility treatments, and I had never even *seen* a positive pregnancy test.

Until now.

I remember that day in the year 2000 like it was yesterday. It was a Saturday and my husband was watching some college football on TV. I remember walking directly in front of him and holding up the two tests without saying a word. "What is that?" he asked. I said, "It's two pregnancy tests that say I'm pregnant." Without even missing a beat or bothering to take his eyes off the TV, he said, "Honey, you know you're not. Those things are never accurate."

WHAT? I mean, really, *what did he just say?!* We had been trying for almost eight years to get pregnant and now I was standing there in front of him, *with proof in my hands*, but my husband's reaction was disbelief and denial? I mean, he didn't even bat an eye and just continued to stuff his face.

Despite his reaction, or lack thereof, I asked him if I could call my mom, but he said no. I didn't need to get my hopes up too soon. And until I went to the doctor and had a "proper" test done, I shouldn't say a word to anyone. He didn't show any emotion. He just kept eating his nachos and watching his game.

Now, before you think he was being horrible and insensitive toward me (which I can understand from how I am telling this part of the story), please remember I told you that he's a facts guy and he has to sit on things for a while before really dealing with them. He's also my voice of reason. Hence, his reaction. Would I have liked for him to stand up and share the moment? Sure. But no, he's not horrible or insensitive. Because trust me, when we finally confirmed it, he told EVERYONE! He was just as overjoyed about it as I was.

But even though I hadn't thought about it until using those tests, I somehow *already knew* I was pregnant. And all of the sudden, I started noticing all the signs. My chest was so sore. And, oh yeah, I *had* been really nauseous for the past week, but I thought it was just my nerves from the stress of my sister almost dying. I have also been really tired recently. But again, I thought it was due to having a very active toddler and taking care of my sister's children while she was recovering. I totally missed the signs up to this point, and by the time we got confirmation that I was pregnant, I was already eight weeks along.

That weekend seemed like it was the longest weekend of my life. I had to go to church on Sunday with all the people who had walked through infertility and adoption with me, and I couldn't say a word.

I watched the minutes and seconds on the clock so I could call my doctor's office immediately when they opened on Monday morning. I told them what had happened, but they said they couldn't see me until Wednesday. And with that knowledge, my head and heart were both screaming, "THERE IS NO WAY I AM WAITING UNTIL WEDNESDAY!"

My aunt was a nurse at a general practitioner's office. She would do a test for me if I asked. I called her, told her what had happened, and Matt drove me to her office. She did the test and confirmed that I was, indeed, very much pregnant. Six years of failed infertility treatments, eight years of waiting. God definitely does have a sense of humor.

But my pregnancy was not easy. The morning sickness turned into all-day sickness. At 12 weeks, I started bleeding. And then I passed a huge clot. This had happened to me twice before. "Oh no, no, no. The baby is gone."

That was 21 years ago, and I can still see and remember every single moment of that day. Isn't it crazy how you can have huge gaps in your memory, but some things will just never, ever leave you?

I can still smell the hospital. I can see myself in the wheelchair and being put on that cold sterile bed. I can see myself crying while Matt held my hand. I remember them rolling in the sonogram machine and the sound it made. I remember how uncomfortable it felt. I remember that she turned the screen away from me. I closed my eyes and the tears kept falling.

Then something magical happened. *We heard a heartbeat!*

Noah had been a twin! We didn't know it because the second baby had more than likely already passed when we first found out I was pregnant and the tiny sack had been hiding behind Noah. But what do you do with information like this? There's nothing you can do about your condition at this stage. You're happy because you know that you're still pregnant, but you still recognize the loss of what could have been with another soul joining your family. I simultaneously mourned and rejoiced. It was all I could do. And looking back, I chose to be happier for my situation at that moment. There was, after all, still plenty of joy to be thankful for.

If you haven't guessed it by now, I delivered a healthy baby boy at 37 weeks and we named him Noah. He came early, and just like Noah in the Bible, he came in on a storm, in the very literal sense. In addition to that, his birth was traumatic and I came very close to dying. At one point, the doctor didn't know if Noah would make it either, but there were angels in that room that day. I guess I hadn't run over all of them in my irresponsible car ride a couple years earlier.

However, six months after he was born, on December 18, 2001 (our wedding anniversary, no less), I had an emergency hysterectomy. My body was never able to fully recover from the traumatic events of his birth. So, in a nutshell, at the age of 30, I had lost a child, birthed a child, and lost the ability to ever have another.

Noah was only six months old at the time. But ever since his birth, I had to reckon with the fact that he was a very sickly baby. He suffered from colic and he cried nonstop. He also developed chronic ear infections that resulted in him requiring surgery just two weeks before my hysterectomy. And let's not forget that I also had a 3-year-old with autism. I was barely holding it all together.

I wish I could tell you that we all lived happily ever after. Because at 30 years old, after eight years of marriage, I had endured more pain and personal trials than most people experience in their entire lifetime. But no, there would be more hard times. And I was so broken that I felt I had reached my limit. How much more could I possibly take?

I really should have learned to never ask that question.

A few months before, on September 11, 2001, four planes took off and life changed as we knew it. As a result, Matt was laid off from his job. He was in the hospitality and travel industry and no one was traveling. We found ourselves with a 3-year-old, a newborn, and no job. I was having major complications from Noah's birth and was facing surgery and we were at a loss of what to do. After a few months, they gave Matt the option of coming back to the company but he would be transferred to another property that required us to move six hours away from our family.

Matt's new job had him working more than 50 hours a week while I was taking care of two very challenging and demanding babies and recovering from surgery.

It was not supposed to be this way.

I was in a new town with no friends and no family nearby. I was trying to be happy with what God had given me, but in the span of six months, my body had birthed a child and then went through menopause twenty years too early. I had severe postpartum depression and had no idea. That is, until the day when I realized it, and it was almost too late.

Remember what I said earlier about having nine lives? Well, I'm about to tell you about the second time I almost took my life, and with it the lives of my children. All I really remember of that day is driving. Noah was crying. And crying. And crying. And Mari-Kate was screaming too because she couldn't handle the noise that Noah was making. I could see that the lane I was driving in was really just a road on top of an embankment with a steep downward slope off to the right, resembling a cliff with water down below. And it just looked so calm and serene. A voice from somewhere was telling me to take a hard right and drive right into it because then I would have peace. Everything would be quiet, and that would make everything okay again. I almost believed it.

It's so easy to judge those mothers who kill themselves and their babies. We automatically assume they must be the most horrible, unpredictable, and emotionally distorted people in the world. It's also the same way we label people who "commit" suicide. We, as members of society, believe that they are little more than selfish people who would take their own lives, or the lives of others, as if they didn't recognize anything of value in the world.

But these are people you see every day. They sit beside you at church. They smile at you in the supermarket. You compliment them on how adorable their children are. And they nod and say thank you. That was me. I looked every bit of that lovely, wonderful, stereotypical mom who thought being a mother was the greatest gift in the world. But, inside there's something you don't see or even suspect. These people are secretly suffering. *I* was secretly suffering. I loved my children with all my heart. I had gone through so much to even have them in my life. But that day, I saw death as the only way to get peace.

But thankfully, my angels came to my rescue and saved me once again.

Maybe it was my heart pounding. Or maybe it was my nervous system shutting down. Maybe it was waking up! I didn't know. What I did know was that I could feel my inner being getting shaken like an earthquake to wake up from this terrible nightmare. And I didn't drive off the edge of that road. Somehow my angels guided me as I was driving and I ended up at my doctor's office with both of my children in my arms, cascades of tears flooding down my face, and begging for help.

That day could have turned out so, so differently. Oh, but for the grace of God, because they immediately took me into a room and called my husband. The next day I was in therapy and on a new medication. I was diagnosed with post-traumatic stress disorder and a severe case of depression.

Depression is real, my friend. And if you have even the slightest suspicion of anyone close to you being at risk, you need to check on your people because it's usually the ones who show no physical signs who may have it the worst. Not one person in my life *ever* saw the signs of depression in me, and I had been suffering from it since I was 15 years old.

I do want to stop here for just a moment, though, and give some praise to the breadth and virtually immediate effects of Prozac. In many ways it's a God-sent invention, and I'm so thankful that He gave someone the wisdom to create the drug that helps me function on a daily basis. I still take it every day and truly wouldn't be alive without it. I should make a T-shirt that reads, "Jesus + Prayers + Prozac." I could be a millionaire. Maybe I missed my calling. Don't you steal my idea though!

I want to make it very clear that Christians and "happy people" do get depressed. And it's not a lack of faith or any kind of "God problem" that is the cause. We need to stop this narrative. Depression is a *disease*. And some personalities are more prone to its grip. But let me say with extreme clarity, *it is not a weakness.*

So yes, of course, praise God and praise Jesus. Forever and ever, amen. And praise Prozac too. It's not something you can have a relationship with, like God and Jesus, but it's certainly on the list of things that change your life for the better when your circumstances warrant it. I will never be ashamed of taking medications that bring me back to me.

Let's take another pause.

Friend, I know you just had to endure some really dark and difficult moments of my life. Maybe it triggered you somewhat. For that, I'm truly very sorry. But I didn't write this book just to bring you through all the hard times in my life or drag you through all my dirt in order to make you feel sad or sorry for me. I brought you through this because all of this happened for a divine reason. It is what has led me to where I am today. And yes, it's all part of *my* story, but I now know that there are plenty of people who can identify with my plight and who may need to see how someone else coped, persevered, and succeeded past it. That's the real mission here.

And I will probably never understand why, but when bad things happen to me, it always forces me to doubt my faith or at least *want to*. I will never understand why people are taken from us too soon. Why do some people seem to have the best of life, while others of us have to endure incredible pain and hardships? The old phrase, "The grass is always greener" comes to mind often, but that certainly doesn't explain anywhere close to everything we feel when we are insecure about something. It's not jealousy or envy or anything else that I can put my finger on. Maybe it's just *life*. Maybe life itself has to test its own boundaries while using us as a vehicle to see where it can thrive and where it doesn't want to go again. But, as a believer, I know that everything I have gone through was to bring me to my higher purpose of what I'm supposed to do with the rest of my life. And sometimes it takes us 50 years to get here.

PART 1:
CHAPTER 5

THE RISE AND FALL

"Just about anything will work again
if you just hit reset."

Julie Paisley

I've had two major careers in my lifetime. I've been a teacher and I've been a photographer. Those two parts of my life couldn't be more different. The teacher years found us in the trenches of infertility and then raising young children. We were living from paycheck to paycheck, awkwardly trying to find our way as we navigated being married and being parents.

We had seven years of just us, but within a span of two years, we had two children, complete with two big moves and all of the life that goes with that. It's hard to remember everything during this part of my life. I think some days you just survive. Raising small children and being a wife is the greatest privilege, but it's also the hardest job I've ever had.

As a mom, I think you start to lose some of your identity. You are known as someone's mom or someone's wife, and you are no longer just yourself. The world revolves around those little people who make messes but give the sweetest kisses.

After Noah was born, it was hard for me to be a stay-at-home mom. *Very hard.* I was not one of those Pinterest, Betty Crocker moms. I loved working and after all the trauma of the past few years, I needed to feel valued to feel whole. I'm not saying that is a good quality of mine, but it came from all the years of feeling like I had to be performing and showing how valuable I was to society. I never felt that just being me and being a mom was enough. So, when Noah turned four, I went back to teaching.

I was super fortunate. I was a teacher at the private school that was associated with our church, and although I was working, I had the same hours as the kids. I loved going back to work. It fulfilled me. I felt seen and valuable again.

I had gotten used to the high from the outward validation and it felt good. Because when I was praised, I felt like I had purpose. But I also had this sick desire to do more and to be better. Why was that praise and a pat on the back so important to me?

It's like a disease. You convince yourself that all this giving and working hard while people-pleasing is making you out to be a saint. But no. It's making you a doormat and that is why people start walking all over you. It's crazy how the lines get crossed.

Why do we, as women, think we are nothing without outward validation? We have to be skinny, dress well, be the perfect mom, and the perfect wife. It's like an evil and secret competition that we moms have with each other. Do we want to be the best wife we can be for our husbands? Sadly, no. Most of us do it because we want other people to see that we are a wonderful wife. Why do we need the big fancy house? Or drive new vehicles? Well, you all know the answer to that.

Also, do you really believe the lie that we buy that beautiful new dress to wear to church to please God? NOPE. So far from it. It's for attention. Because we need it to feel valuable and validated. It's in us all. And it is a cycle that will probably never be broken. Especially in this age of social media, keeping up with the Joneses will always be something that the masses will have to contend with.

But I hope that by you reading this book, you will start to realize that we don't NEED any of those things to be valuable and worthy, no matter what people say. Because trust me, *I know.*

I'm sure you remember reading back at the beginning of this book when I went on to explain how the pressure of trying to be perfect almost took everything away from me. Well, Friend, I certainly did try to live that perfect life. But if you think it was bad during my teenage and college years, put on your seatbelt because it's about to get bumpy.

Yes, this precious, beautiful life that God had called me to was almost lost due to feeling like I was not enough, no matter how blessed I was with genuine gifts from God. I once again started believing the lie that I was flawed and unworthy to walk this earth.

I found comfort in material things, how people perceived me, and my accomplishments. These were things that made me feel valuable and seen. I felt seen when I was at the top. It's all we really want, right? To be seen and loved.

But getting to the top is not without sacrifice, and I learned in 2021 that the sacrifice was not worth it anymore if I wanted to live. And I *did* want to live. But not only did I want to live, I also wanted to thrive. And above all else, I was determined to make sure that as long as I walked this earth, my purpose would be to help others before they got to where I was in November of 2021. Because no one should ever stare down at a handful of pills and feel like life would be better if they were not in it. I remember that old song we used to sing in Sunday School that went:

> *"Red and Yellow,*
> *Black and White,*

They are so, so precious
In His sight."

If only I had paid more attention to that song when I was kid. It's amazing what the years will do to one's perspective. And as much as it pains me to write about what happened next, I'm going to be honest and vulnerable. I'm revealing thoughts and struggles that I have never even spoken out loud, though I'm pretty sure there may be some notes in one of my old journals. Maybe I didn't understand the notes I had written in it. Were those journal entries written by that girl in the mirror? *Hmm.* In either case, I had certainly never put those thoughts on display for all the world to see.

But it's time.

If this whole project of my heart and mind helps just one single person, it will all be worth it in my eyes. Because this part of my story needs to be told. Because I'm still here. And not everyone gets that privilege. I was one of the fortunate ones. All the struggles in my life brought me to this place. And what happened next is why I'm writing this book in the first place. It really is for those of you who are experiencing similar struggles and frustrations. *It is for you* that I'm sharing my story.

On the outside, I had it all. People envied me—or at least they wanted the best parts of what they believed was my lifestyle. I spent my whole life getting to this level of success and accomplishments. But the years and years of people-pleasing and not living my true self had brought me to complete burnout. I was a volcano about to explode. The date was May 28th, 2021.

I was back in Nashville for doctor's appointments that I had put on hold for years because I was too busy becoming successful to take care of myself. Work was slowly starting to come back after a year of cancellations, and I was beginning to accept that things would never again be the way they were. There had been a worldwide break in continuity but I was actually okay with that.

A few days before, we received the news that my father-in-law now had terminal leukemia in addition to bladder cancer. On that same day, my daughter's cat suddenly died from a stroke. She's autistic. *That cat was the world to her.*

I was crushed. It seemed my perfect world was falling apart again. I was going through all these tests and appointments alone because my husband was with his family, dealing with the fact that his dad was given less than six months to live. I was also alone in a hotel room when I received the news that would hit me like a piano falling out of the sky, leaving a crater in my perspective.

Modern technology is great. We learn about things instantly. But sometimes, that modern convenience can be bad. Like really, really bad.

It was Friday night at around six. I had just ordered DoorDash because, really, who wants to eat alone at a restaurant unless you're there to explore some big, exciting city on a summer day? And quite frankly, it had already been a week from hell with all the bad news. Add to that being poked and prodded from all the appointments, which was a whole bunch of no fun. In fact, just three days prior, I had six biopsies done for possible skin cancers and was still nursing those stitches. I had big plans for the weekend, which included staying in my sweatshirt and leggings, binge-watching Netflix while ordering DoorDash, and eating through the stack of comfort food from my latest run to Target. I just wanted to disappear from social media and everyone else. I wanted to have some "me time" while I tried to wrap my head around all the changes that would be happening, and were already happening, in our lives.

I was smiling on the outside and playing the part of a successful business owner. But inside, I was falling apart. Again. And then my phone dinged. I picked it up and there was notification from my health app saying I had new test results. I really didn't think anything of it because I had so much bloodwork done the past week that it didn't even dawn on me that it could be the pathology report from the biopsies. So, I clicked and opened it up. And then I saw it. There it was. Written in bold, red letters were the words, "Malignant Melanoma."

At first, I didn't even see that it wasn't only one of the biopsies that was cancerous. No. It was ALL SIX. I remember feeling dizzy because I think I was holding my breath. My brain was on fast forward. I had a rescheduled trip to Europe for work in four weeks. I had ten rescheduled weddings in August, September, and October and they were all in destination locations. My father-in-law was just given up to six months to live and we were temporarily moving to Ohio because he needed full-time care. And now I have cancer too? Another C word. Can we please just erase that letter from our alphabet? What in the world was happening?

My head was racing. *I couldn't have cancer.* My business was the sole provider of income for my family. If I didn't work, we didn't eat or pay our bills. We were in the process of moving to Ohio to care for my dying father-in-law. I HAD to work because Matt couldn't right now. What if I needed chemo? What if I had to cancel all the work that was on my schedule? How would we survive? What if I don't survive? My husband is going to lose his father *and* his wife? Oh, and my son is in college. How could we afford it *now*? And as for the medical bills, we had insurance, but self-employed insurance really sucks. I'm a leader in my industry. What will people think? I will lose all my clients because no one will hire someone with cancer and who may be unreliable as a result. I had worked so hard to be successful in my field and now I was going to lose it all.

For those of you reading this who may be wondering—if you are familiar with the Enneagram personality profiling system, I'm a number 2, wing 3, which is the "Helper" with strong influences from the "Achiever" category. And just like all Helpers, I immediately charged forward to figure out how to solve this and to take care of it all because that's "just what Helpers do." But I also went into survival mode for everyone else, totally disregarding myself because that's "just what Achievers tend to do." I don't want to get too much into it here but Enneagram profiling is a well-respected system that allows people to understand their character traits as processed and manifested through their psyche. I am a big fan of it. Not only because it allowed me to know where my strengths and weaknesses were, but it allowed me to know where my strengths could and could not make up for my weaknesses. And *that* is pretty valuable information.

Anyway, there I was, facing cancer, and all I could think about was my business and my career? *I've* got to be kidding myself! And looking back on that now, I am so ashamed.

Being successful and keeping my status was more important to me than my own life. And you want to know why? Because I wasn't living *my* success, I was living HERS. I had been living my whole life based on what others were doing and the expectations of those people. I had slowly been killing myself in my life and in my business for everyone else, and now it was too late. I was the one who needed saving, but I couldn't save myself. I was a person who needed outward validation to survive and my business gave me that. Without it, I was nothing. It was my identity. I had become addicted to how I was perceived by those around me. By my own self-image. Shameful.

I think that, perhaps, many of us have somehow convinced ourselves that we cannot be successful on our own. We constantly compare ourselves to others and think we need to follow this certain path for our success, just like all of the "sheeple" ahead of us.

But there is a huge problem with that. *We* are not *them.* And although we try to copy, rinse, repeat, and then move on to the next newest, brightest thing, it ends up being self-defeating. We think, "It's obviously working for them. It will work for me too." But it's a dangerous cycle in this entrepreneurial life. It puts us on a seemingly endless hamster-wheel that is constantly spinning and never stops to let us off.

That is, until the circuit breaks. And then the power shuts down from overload, so the wheel won't spin until it gets reset. And it may even need to cool down for a while too.

And the only person who can reset that breaker is the person in the room. And usually, that breaker box is not easy to get to. It's in the basement or behind a stack of things in a closet. That reset button is put out of sight for a reason because it's ugly and we want to hide it, pretending it's not there. But Friend, take this little lesson to heart—just about anything will work again once you hit reset.

The following week after my diagnosis was a veritable whirlwind, like a gust of wind that had grown large enough to audition for tornado alley. There were too many details, too many specific times and locations, and too many fears and emotions to sift through, let alone comprehend. Surgery got scheduled within a week. I had six cancers, and two of them would require major surgery. One of them could require multiple surgeries, and depending on what they found when they went in, it could even require chemo or radiation. I went in for the first surgery on June 8th. Two days before my 50th birthday and ironically on my son's birthday.

The larger of the tumors that needed to be removed was right in the middle of my back along my spine. I ended up with 38 stitches inside and out. But two days later, on my 50th birthday, we received the news that they had removed all the cancer. I've never been more grateful for anything in my life. One down. I still had five more cancers to be removed, one requiring another surgery, and the other four requiring minor procedures. But the worst cancer, the big melanoma, was gone. Best birthday present ever!

As you have read in my story so far, you've become familiar with what I have endured in my life. I think I can say that I'm pretty tough. I have learned how to cope. And by coping, what I really mean is that I dismiss it and continue on with life. I wrap it up in a pretty little bow and I put it deep in the attic. This was how I handled my cancer and all the other hard things that were going on. I simply pretended they weren't there. And within one week of my surgery, I was on a plane back to work and returning to the grind. I didn't even take the time to process it.

Within two weeks of my surgery, I was shooting a wedding in so much pain that I collapsed for two days afterwards. And within three weeks of my surgery, I was headed to Europe for two weeks to teach a workshop. "If I just ignore the situation, it will all go away, right?" I just couldn't stop. My work had become my drug of choice and I had a serious addiction.

In addition to my health problems, my business was in serious danger. Because so much work had been postponed in 2020, 80% of my income had already been paid out the year before. I was in no shape to bring in new money because my personal life was pure hell. I was also in survival mode with extreme burnout. And please take it to heart when I tell you that *you cannot make money in burnout.*

So, what did I do? Instead of trusting God, I decided to fix it all myself. I made terrible choices. More than I care to admit. And for the first time ever, my business was in debt.

I felt there was no other way. I couldn't let anyone see that I was suffering and think less of me. I had to keep up the silly façade and I just would not ask for help. I was Julie Paisley. People knew who I was. I could not show my failure.

But I was falling apart and now my business was falling apart because I could not physically and mentally keep up with it. I was drowning, barely keeping my head above water. I started hating it. I dreaded waking up each morning to do my job. I procrastinated. I stopped answering emails. My heart was no longer in it.

This thing that had brought me so much success and joy was literally sucking the life out of me. I returned home from Europe thoroughly exhausted and harboring way too much anxiety. I was having panic attacks on a daily basis that I hid from everyone. I would go on social media, put on a good show, and then go cry it all out. I had major imposter syndrome. I felt like a liar and a fake. I constantly lived in fear that someone was going to discover the truth and ruin my business forever. But thankfully, no one knew because I looked happy online and I was so good at pretending. In fact, I was better at pretending than being my true self. Or maybe I just didn't even know who my true self was.

I made it through June. And now that it was July, it was time for my second surgery. I was only going to have a week to recover before my next wedding. I sold myself on the lie that I didn't have a choice.

However, this surgery was harder than the first because there were thirty-something stitches in my shoulder and they had to cut through muscle. This type of cancer was deep because I had ignored it for years. Not pleasant. But it didn't matter. I couldn't stop and I wasn't going to.

On top of everything, my father-in-law took a turn for the worse and ended up in the hospital for four weeks. At the end of the four weeks, they sent him home with only 2-4 weeks to live and it was time for us to move in with them full-time. Remember that RV we bought to travel the states? We had been living in it on a farm since April. Crazy how God knew we didn't need a house or a mortgage during this difficult time so we could be in Ohio to care for Dad. But now he needed overnight care. We sent Mari-Kate to live with my parents in Florida because there just wasn't enough room for all of us to live in their tiny apartment. We were surrounded by emotional chaos, and somehow, I was there mentally juggling the details of my business life too. I still had to shoot eight more weddings *and* run a conference before the end of the year. Much of the time, all I could feel was the guilt of not being with family when they needed me the most. I had so much guilt that the guilt itself was an unhealthy fact of my life.

I thought that I had gone through burnout before. I think we may all become "worn out" from time to time in our professional lives. However, I'm going to tell you the difference between being worn out and having burnout. If you are simply worn out, with a little oil here and a little oil there, and maybe even a little TLC, you can keep going. True burnout, though, is when all the wires are fried and smoke is coming out of your ears and nostrils. You suddenly pause for a moment and *poof.* You have the inescapable realization that you are willing to walk away from everything in order to survive.

My burnout had been building for 12 years. I had devoted myself to a business in an industry that was never there for "me" in any meaningful way in the first place. I had sacrificed my family, my health, and my true self to people who only wanted a piece of me when I was at the top. Surprisingly, at first anyway, all of those "best friends" in the industry were nowhere to be found.

They removed me from their text groups and I felt so alone. I felt used and discarded. All these years I had been so concerned about what the industry thought of me, and now when I needed them the most and thought I had earned a little reciprocation, they had moved on. Or more accurately, they had *moved away*, at least emotionally. The very people who I had been supporting and killing myself for didn't even see that I was dying. *They didn't want to.* It turned out that the only people that actually checked in on me were beautiful souls that I had never met in person but who followed me on social media.

For the first time ever, I realized that this business that I had lost myself to was not worth all the sacrifice. But I was in too deep. I had to make drastic changes. I had passed the point of no return. The only way out was to finish what I had committed to and walk away.

I would lose the money, the fame, and everything that went with the lifestyle. I would no longer be special anymore. I would just be Julie. A 50-year-old failure. This could bankrupt my family. I might lose my marriage. My reputation would be ruined. It would just be easier to leave this world before anyone found out. And on November 9th, 2021, it almost happened.

I laid on the bathroom floor, sobbing in the fetal position with a mound of pills in my hand. At that moment, I had two choices. Take the pills and leave this earth or accept that I needed help, ask for it, and do the work. But the latter would be so hard. I've had enough hardship in my life and I was so tired. It would be easier to just go to sleep and never wake up. I didn't want the world to see that I had failed. Life felt just so dang hard.

But God wasn't finished with me yet. It was time for me to live HIS purpose and not live a life based on achievements and someone else's success anymore. It's been almost a year now from that day and I'm so glad I chose to live.

Has it been easy? Nope. Not at all.

But has it been worth it? YES! So much so. Yes.

I had worked for 13 years to get my business to the top. I did "all things necessary." But it was time to give it all up and start again from the bottom. And for the first time in my life, I actually welcomed the change. It had to be this way. I was no longer at the point where I could just slow down. No, I let myself pass that chance years ago.

This required a full shut-down. Because sometimes we have to stop in order to start again. And that is just what I did. I found my own version of success and I found it on *my* terms with what felt *right*. I turned off all the noise and I only listened to God and to what He was telling my heart.

And so now we can get to the good part, the part of how I did it. This is where grace and hope come in. And if you have related to any part of my story, this is where I'm giving you permission to start over too. It's not rocket science. And you can do this too because it's never too late to be the person who you were meant to be. I'm living proof because I am now 51 years old and I feel like my life is *just beginning*.

So, you see, I told you that this book was not all doom and gloom, and that there is a light at the end of the tunnel. It actually ends on a happy note with a lesson on how you can overcome burnout, stop living the imposter life, and build a life and business that truly brings you joy and purpose.

I don't have it all figured out yet, but I know I will always be developing. I continue to be a work-in-progress, but I have found my new purpose. And for the first time in my life, I don't wake up every day needing outward validation to feel loved and valuable. In fact, most days I never even feel the need to look at Instagram for any reason other than pure business. And if it weren't required for the type of business I operate, I wouldn't have any need to be on it at all anymore. It's no longer a place where I go to feel okay about myself. I don't look at likes and shares and follows. I use Instagram to help others now, not for outward validation.

I know that the first part of this book was hard but I hope you can understand why I felt I had to share all of the hard with you first. I needed to share my struggles and mistakes because those are the things that laid the foundation for my healing. Moreover, I believe that's the way it is for everyone. The things that we struggle with and work through are the building blocks for our real fortresses. They *had* to happen so that I could reflect on them in a way that enlightened me to the desire of helping others with their own piles of rubble. God knows that I had to deal with mine, and He showed me how to put them into place to make me stronger and to live without the puppet strings. God puts us all through hard times for the simple fact that we can help others not feel so alone. I truly believe that that was my purpose. God chose for me to have this journey and I feel so honored to have come out on the other side. I know that God loved me so much that He allowed me to endure all of these things in order to get this message out.

And now, what I used to believe was a curse has become my greatest weapon. Because, on the receiving end, it's different when someone tries to help you when they truly know how you feel. It makes me think of the old expression, "People don't care how much you know until they know how much you care." And when someone has shared a similar experience of true hardship, they're going to care. In fact, they're going to care so much that you'll know. *You'll just know.*

Do I have all the answers? Nope, not even close. Only God does. But I can certainly relate and feel your pain. I refuse to let my story and all those hard times end in vain. And for the rest of my life, I have made a vow to God to be His vessel through which He heals others. And now it's your turn to heal.

Can I personally heal you? No. Can I help you and give you some suggestions? Yes. But you are going to have to do the work and make some serious changes in your life. Are you ready? If so, let's go.

PART 2

THE HEALING

PART 2:
CHAPTER 1

NEW BEGINNINGS

INTRODUCTION

My Dear Friend,

Thank you for getting through all of that with me. I know there was a lot of emotion swimming around in those chapters. And I know most, if not all of you, can relate to my struggle in your own personal way, to some degree or another. Men included. Whatever struggle you've endured, whether noticed or unnoticed by others, is still *an event* in your life that commanded some or all of your attention for an important amount of time. And everyone has "their way" of dealing with, or not dealing with, their personal challenges.

Some people are just lucky and can simply shrug things off more easily than others, but they still struggle like we all do. Of course, maybe they haven't had any "critical" issues to deal with *yet*, so they may not be "bothered" by anything at a core level. On the other hand, maybe they have *already had* some critical issues happen and got through them! And now, those people just might not be that bothered anymore. So, don't judge a book by its cover.

Then there are other people who internalize all of their challenges at a *much* deeper level and severely battle with their circumstances. To you, they may often seem preoccupied or possibly even distant. But to them, their struggles are their reality in moment-to-moment, daily obligations or routines. And if you are one of those people, you can feel like a real (fill in the blank).

The point is, everyone needs genuine, honest help at different points in life. But the catch is, and please pay attention here, in order to get the help that they truly need at their very core, at least one of two things absolutely must happen. Either they need to find a way to ask for whatever help they need or they need to be able to recognize help when it is being offered. And in both cases, it starts with a simple conversation. That's kind of what I have been trying to have with you here. A conversation. And yes, I know, I've been doing all the talking, but writing this has been helping me to help you. This has been me sharing with you some extremely personal events in my life that really messed me up. And because the very act of writing this has been helping me get past them, the very act of you reading this book has been helping you relate to it for reasons that you will see shortly.

And in that sense, we've been building a relationship this whole time. That's why I try to write, most of the time anyway, as if I were sitting in a room talking with you. It's the very reason why I keep calling you Friend. At the beginning of this book, I invited you into my life as a friend and I truly meant it. We all need friends. And frankly, we could probably all use at least a few more really good ones.

But this part of the book is going to be a bit different. Up to now you've been reading my story. Part two is more about you using your story to begin working on a process. It's about turning all that rubble into a strong emotional foundation, building your real fortress, and turning your weaknesses into weapons so that you can defend yourself when future struggles make their way to your drawbridge. Because rest assured, they are coming. But don't let that worry you.

In the upcoming pages, we'll talk about some important but simple and reasonable principles. And I have already said that healing begins with a conversation. Well, who is starting the conversation? Are you the one asking? Or are you the one recognizing that help is being offered? That's something to think about.

In either case, maybe, probably, absolutely that conversation should begin with God. Try to lift even an eyelid and be open to the influence that God is always trying to find a way to really, *really*, **really** reach you. And if you choose to answer that call, I hope my experience has played some role in you finding that choice to be the right one. And if that conversation is not to take place at this time, I hope you keep going forward in that conversation with yourself. That is, your *self.* You'll see what I mean a little later.

This part of the book is much shorter than the first, and this is by design. You may think, "Um, why? I've cried all the way here." Well, I ask you to consider that maybe it's because the remedy should always be easier to handle than whatever caused the problem. But aside from that, I also ask you to consider that you are now already awake to the pitfalls of stored-up trauma. So, let's try to get us both out of this trap little by little. Just one small step at a time. That's what I am offering. You've helped *me* and now I want to help *you.*

At a certain point during my very thankful recovery from that whole mess, I was able to identify the key elements of the healing process that I spent the greatest amount of time thinking about. Believe me, I spent *a lot* of time thinking about these things. And once I found the right word for each of those little puzzle pieces, I tried to organize those thoughts so that I could always remember them easily. That way, I could always recognize if something was missing in my path forward. So, I made a silly little acronym to unite the main points. I even giggled when it came to me, because it represents one of the most significant driving forces in our personalities. And what I found, quite literally, was *success*.

S - Self

U - Unity

C - Community

C - Clarity

E - Enjoyment

S - Stillness

S - Satisfaction

I think you'll see that I am going to come around full circle on a number of things. I spent quite a bit of time in the introduction talking about a lot of little things that made me *me* at the time. Or at least, that's what I thought. Now that we've gotten through the story part, it's time to put those big-girl panties on again and start discovering and discussing what we've learned. I decided to make this chapter the second introduction to this book. Maybe you already noticed. And if you're going to be able to repair, heal, and become well, you need to understand and *grasp* what is coming at you so that it doesn't interfere with your ability to focus on the goal.

The next chapter will be the longest of these chapters because it deals with the self. If you really think about it on a deeper level, you find that *you* and *yourself* are much bigger than just the sum of your parts. Even on a molecular level and it's because we have a soul. There is, quite literally, someone in there. And the simple fact that we have a soul is God's evidence screaming at us that we were designed for all of this. There is just *so much* about us as human individuals that turns our bodies into carriers of that inner person. And on top of that, we are extremely complex things. Not just as people or living organisms, but as individual, life-bearing, caring, and thinking personalities in a body with an expiration date that we are not supposed to know.

And that's why the Bible is still so important today. It is not just a book that has lasted longer than every empire in the history of the world. No. It's a collection of books. It's *the original* collection of books. And by itself, it's a small library of the most important philosophical concepts *ever*. Yes, ever! And it's not because *I* say so. There is a huge, unknowable number of books, articles, movies, college thesis papers, etc. that have been written about the Bible in the course of history. The history of thinking is contained in that library. By definition, that includes all of our philosophies, values, wonders, and reasons for faith.

The complexity of our bodies is enough to make you stagger. Then add to that the complexity of our circumstances. We all have moments, events, and times that test us when we feel vulnerable enough already. But please, notice that I am using the word complex, not complicated. Believe me, I know that things do get complicated for all of us. But it's only because we allow them to. And truly, that's usually because we're trying to avoid them. Friend, I'm telling you from my heart, we need to learn how to face our struggles head-on. *Complexity* is less likely to become *complicated* when you are prepared for what you are getting into. So, you need to get to know that person in the mirror because, like it or not, you are looking at *yourself*. But not only that, you need to know how to take care of it, as well as anticipate its needs.

And to further highlight the complex side of things, every single one of us, in our individual brains, has nearly a hundred billion interacting neurons. Our brains are our own personal universes! What better place for God to live with us! And to avoid getting complicated, let's suffice to say that neurons are like tiny little sensors that never stop communicating with all of our experiences. All the past ones. All the present ones. And all the future ones. *Simultaneously!*

With modern-day research, we understand that these neurons obviously communicate with our right-here-and-now experiences, because that's how we interact in moment-to-moment life. But they also communicate with our past ones. And that is what forms our learned behaviors. These learned behaviors become what we apply to our ability to control our possible outcome, or our future. And even though you can't get it right every time, when you focus on the desired future, you learn how to get better at shaping it. Tomorrow's view of next week should be clearer than yesterday's view of it, right? And *that* is what makes your vision of your future sharper, brighter, better, and much more fulfilling.

Please, if you need to, go ahead and read that last paragraph again. Just to make sure you got it. Because to me, this is proof that the soul is always seeking its needs. It will encounter many desires, pleasures, and even miserable hardships along the path. But it will always be seeking its needs. So, when you begin to recognize how to give structure to a small portion of your future, your soul gets to start looking for what will fulfill it. And that's what imagination is. You are not predicting your future—you're beginning to shape it. And once you start to see a shape that you actually like, you begin *needing* to work on it more. But now it's with a little more passion than before.

In a nutshell, you are able to take all of your learned behaviors to deal with the right-here-and-now in order to imagine what the future could be and begin making a series of small decisions that bring your imagined future closer to you. That is truly amazing!

And with each successful decision, you are able to breathe a little sigh of completion that has prepared you for the next decision. Just like graduation is not defined as only completing high school or college, graduation is also called commencement, or a new beginning. It's a repeating cycle that everyone can ride. And when you learn how, it's fun.

The next chapter is about self, and because we, as humans, are so complex, I have devoted more time to that topic. I believe you will see why taking care of the self will help you take care of everything else. And now that you know *my* story, I want you to focus on your own story and extract what you need in order to help and heal *you*.

I told you earlier that I was a teacher in my first career. I believe that it truly is my calling, and probably always has been. I don't feel called to go back to teaching students in grade school, or even college for that matter. But I do feel like I'm called to teach to my fellow entrepreneurs. It's what I believe will lead me to all my future joys. And that means my very purpose for the rest of my life is to help people find rest, bring joy back into their business, find ways to support their efforts, and show them that success is personal and not based on what others think success should be for them.

And truthfully, we can all have our own success. Because we all view things differently, you need to define what that means to you and make it personal. Something that lifts you. Something that no one else has any controlling influence over. Of course, that doesn't mean you won't want or need influence. Much of it can be very positive. But the key is that no one should have any *control* over what your inner self is looking for except you.

Your success could very well be making millions of dollars and living all over the world in luxury. Or your success could be being a great wife and mom and living in the same place your entire life. Either way, it doesn't matter because each is just as important as the other. There are no concrete measures of success when we realize that our own success is exclusive to every individual. And even though I find myself rethinking all about the lies I, or we, have endured up to now, I have to plant my flag on these concepts.

I was so deep in burnout that I had two choices. I could remove myself from this life or I could remove the lie! My job had become my own personal hell and it wasn't because of the people. I loved my clients and my fellow photographers. But now, through all of this, I realized that *I* had to be at least one of the priorities in my life so that I could reach others effectively. It was time to make drastic changes. So, I walked away from a career that I loved so I could find myself again. Sometimes that's the only choice we are left with in order to heal.

And, for the first time in 13 years, there are no weddings in my books and that brings me so much peace. I don't need to be a famous photographer to be worthy. I am worthy all on my own.

So let's get into it, because this is how I healed. This is how I found my way to Becoming Julie. That's Julie. Not Super Julie. Not Celebrity Photographer Julie. Just Julie. Because just being Julie is enough for me.

PART 2: CHAPTER 2

S = SELF

I do not find it ironic that the first letter of my little acronym turned out to be the letter "S" for *Self*. You'll recall that in the previous chapter, I mentioned that taking care of that thing we call "self" will help you take care of other aspects of your life. So, let's dive in.

Before I could even think about rebuilding my business, I had to take care of myself first. That is to say, *my self*, with an emphasis on both parts. You see, we always say the word "myself" the way it is used in everyday life. But I think it's one of those important words that is sometimes necessary to break down to separate components in order to reveal a more valuable and more complete meaning. So, let's take a look at them.

First let's ask, when do we say *my*? Well, we use it to denote *ownership*, like when I refer to *my* cameras and photography equipment. We also say it to indicate *control* over something, as in *my* hands, feet, car, schedule, etc. But we also use it to represent *access* to something, like *my* emotions, thoughts, and memories. Right away, you begin to see some things are just more personal than others. And then . . . We also say it to identify relationships like *my* husband, mother, father, sister, brother, friend, coworker, professor, etc. And yes, when you say *myself*, you are in fact stating that you have a relationship with *you*. Does that sound unreasonable? I don't think so at all. So, let's swim a little deeper.

When we use the word "self," we are really talking about an *entity*, in both physical and abstract forms. Our physical self is our body, all the internal organs, and all the processes they use for us to live. And when they stop performing their necessary and intended functions, our physical existence begins to break down. The abstract self, though, is very different. The abstract self is kind of like the wind. You can't see it or even hear it directly. You can, however, perceive its effect on trees, leaves, water, sand, hair, etc. You *know* it's there because you can feel it. But you can't grab or hold it to keep it from going on its journey past you. The abstract self has a set of needs that distinguish it from the physical self. So, for the purposes of this book, let's boil it down to the core principles that have helped me the most.

The self needs order and patterns to develop a useful sense of Clarity. The self needs tranquility to isolate and focus on its passions. I will reveal this amazing concept in Chapter 12, which is about Stillness. The self also needs support, which is why true friends are so irreplaceable. You need a team, and I will discuss this further in the chapter on Community. The self needs a goal. And it needs the whole team to be on board for a sense of Unity. The self needs meaningful distractions from everyday routines to give us a sense of Enjoyment. The self needs progress and affirmation, which leads to Satisfaction. The self needs a conclusive statement of status. And I don't mean one's position in society. No, I mean having an accurate understanding of your current condition and the relevance of that condition to all of your input sources. I think you're going to see what I mean in the epilogue.

So, when we say "myself," what we often really mean is the relationship between the physical and abstract elements of self. It's our ownership and control over the access we have to a relationship with our soul. And *that* is what makes each and every one of us a unique individual!

This is NOT the story. This is the recovery. It's the *healing*. And the moment that you give *your own self* a fair shot at tapping into these principles, the veil between confusion and purpose begins to recede.

After this chapter, I'm going to start it off easy with Unity and Community. They're not really heavy concepts. But after that, things start to get, well . . . kinda heavy. The reason I can say this is because I focused on what *my self* was telling *me*. I listened, and it turns out I am not as quiet as I used to think. I have concluded through the practice of listening as best I can to that inner voice for any sign that God disagrees with me that I really need to unearth what I, Julie, my self was mining for. And when I hit emotional paydirt, I found one of the biggest gems of them all. And that is this: to a very large degree, you have to know who you were in order to know who you are. Sorry, but that is inescapable, and it's not a judgment. It's actually quite beautiful if you think about it because it's really a matter of having continued awareness and a determined focus on your progress toward your destination so that you may have fulfillment.

And this can be so hard for most people, especially if you are a woman. At least, I think. Now, I have no idea what truly goes through a man's head most of the time, but even *they* admit they wouldn't put up with what a woman goes through if we didn't do it for them. And that's not an insult toward men. Men have it rough too. In our modern world, men, as a group, have ever-increasing responsibilities for which they are being recognized less and less.

The point is, we all have a depth to us that no one else will ever see or truly know. That is no one's fault. It's an inherent feature of your soul's personal existence. At the time, for me, being a Christian woman in a society where I shouldn't be so obvious, who was also working through some very serious personal and religious trauma, it was even harder on my mental collection of perceptions to handle. But you *can* get over all of that, or whatever concoction of circumstances you may be dealing with. I did. And the following are some of the things that, although are not rocket science, I decided would be good first steps.

I HAVE ME AND GOD TIME IN THE MORNING.

When I wake up, I take at least thirty minutes for myself and God. I do not jump on social media or email right away. No, those thirty minutes belong to no one but God and me. The first thing that I consciously do is lie in bed and pray. When I give my time to God in the morning, before I deal with anyone or anything else, my day just goes better. I've even restarted a plan to read through the whole Bible in a year. I have a Bible app for convenience, and before my feet hit the floor, I spend time with Him. If religion is "not your thing," I'm not trying to force anything on you. But try to access whatever your source for a spiritual connection may be. For you, perhaps it's breathing, yoga, or some sort of meditation. Use this time to connect with that source. For me, it's God.

And for me, praying doesn't always have to be what you might call "formal." I don't always feel the need to get on my knees to pray. Sometimes I just lie in bed, staring at the ceiling, and talk to Him like He's right there in the room with me, because God has become so personal to me in my healing. For so long, I used to fear Him in an unhealthy way due to religious trauma. But now, He's my loving Heavenly Father, and I look forward to my time spent with Him.

After prayer and reading my Bible, I begin on the functional tasks of the day. I get up, drink water, stretch, breathe, and write out what I want to do for that day. I no longer use a weekly planner. I use a monthly planner, so I can see the big picture, and a daily planner because I've found that I do better with sheets of paper that I can throw away at the end of each day, while my month requires more visualization. If I don't get something done today, I write it on what will be tomorrow's page. This is just my way of completing my daily cycle and avoiding any possible onset of burnout. It helps me focus, and honestly, I really *love* checking off lists. Yep, I'm one of those people, and crossing things off my list is literally one of my favorite things in the world.

I GET DRESSED, COMPLETE WITH HAIR AND MAKEUP EVERY WEEKDAY THAT I'M IN MY OFFICE.

This one is new for me. It's such a simple thing. At first, it was actually a hard one to make a habit. During 2020, I fell into a lazy pattern because I told myself, *"You're not going anywhere. You don't need to get dolled up for anything."* I completely embraced the workday in my PJs, sometimes without a shower, and I could go weeks without "getting ready" for the day. I would shower and just put on another set of PJs. I loved it! I mean, everyone else was doing it, so it was acceptable, Right? Well, no.

Now please don't get me wrong, because I don't believe in vanity. And I don't get ready every day with that in mind. But I can tell you that taking twenty minutes to get out of your PJs, get dressed, and make an effort to look presentable produces a substantial shift in your mindset. We need to tell and show our bodies that it's time to exit the rest stage and enter the work stage of the day. And getting ready does that for me.

As for the weekends—that's a different story. Now that I no longer do weddings, I do not work on weekends and staying in my PJs on a Saturday is totally acceptable. In fact, it's good because, in my home, weekends are for restoring myself and not working.

I SET STRONG BOUNDARIES.

Until recently, I had never set boundaries where work was involved. Of course, I've always had *moral* boundaries. But for work, it was always, "I'm available 24/7 and your wish is my command." Well, by reading this book, you can see that approach didn't work out very well for me. So, I want you to stop right now and repeat this out loud. Say it with me, "I am NOT a machine." Repeat, "I am NOT a machine." Now say it louder for the people in the back, "I am NOT a machine."

Have you ever noticed that technology makes things better *and* worse at the same time? Oh sure, phones, computers, and many other things have improved the quality and efficiency of our day-to-day tools quite significantly. However, they don't necessarily improve our work lives because they disproportionately raise the expectations of those we try to serve. Mentally, we live in a microwave-ready society. Everyone seems to want everything in an instant. But sadly, it is often the case that the faster work is completed, the less valuable it is to both client and provider. But we have the power to change that. Good things take time, and the best things can take a lifetime. It's actually okay to stop work between 3 and 5 o'clock. It's okay to not work on the weekends. It's okay to answer an email tomorrow if you receive it after your office hours. If your clients cannot respect your boundaries, let them go.

Yes, I just went there. *Let them go.*

Your clients are not the CEO of your business—you are! Just because they pay you money for a service or product does not give them permission to run your life. If your clients truly respect you and the work they want from you, they can and will wait for you to respond according to your schedule as a professional. Set up an auto reply at the end of your day. Tell them you appreciate them contacting you and you're excited to get back to them. Because an instant response given during your personal time lets them know that you don't have any boundaries at all. And I promise, many will take advantage of you through this corridor if they can.

I STICK TO A DAILY ROUTINE (AS MUCH AS POSSIBLE).

This can certainly be hard at times. Some weeks I have a busy travel schedule, and I do find that it's much easier to stick to my routine when I'm at home and have a dedicated place to work. I actually find myself yearning for my normal routine when I'm out of my more familiar environment. It's a little crazy how just a year ago, work was such a trigger for me. But now it brings me so much joy and I actually look forward to it every day.

Now, I know everyone's life looks a little different, but sticking to a routine and forming good habits can be a lifesaver, especially if you are recovering from burnout. So, here is my routine when I'm not on the road, and even when I am, I still try to stick to it as much as possible.

After I've had my "Me and God Time", and "Getting Ready Time," I usually get right to work. Mornings are best for me because my brain is fresh and isn't filled with all the accumulated noise that a day can bring. I don't allow any of that into my arena before 1 p.m. My morning time has become my most productive time of the day and I don't want anything or anyone taking away that peace and sense of structure. For you, it might be in the afternoon or evening. But for me, it's the first thing in the morning. And because that time is so precious, I protect it with everything in me!

Once I begin my workday, I usually just do a quick scan through my email and text messages really fast. But I don't stay there. I only look for urgent matters from my team and I come back to the rest of my communications in the afternoon.

If possible, I try to only spend time in written correspondence once a day. Email in particular is a trigger for me because I used to be addicted to checking it constantly. Now, however, I know my boundaries.

Good job, Jules!

I also set clear expectations in my messaging as to when I check email and what to anticipate as a response time. If people don't read it, that is on them. I don't have time to babysit adults.

The next thing I do is record reels for Instagram. Reels do not need to be a lot of work, Friend. I keep a notebook of ideas for these and I record something for two ideas each week, which I save to produce later. I don't scroll through Instagram during the morning time. I just respond to comments on my posts and in my DMs. The only time I scroll on Instagram is for fifteen minutes before and 30 minutes after I make a post so I can keep up with events in my field and interact with others. This helps with my engagement factor and we all know how hard it is to actually *reach* people these days on social media.

Instagram and other platforms can be a huge time trap, and it can be very triggering if you are always trying to over-compare yourself with everyone else. If someone triggers you, mute them. It's that simple. In fact, I went years without following other photographers, even if they were my friends, because I wanted to stay in my own lane and I didn't want to be distracted or distraught by baseless comparisons.

By now, it's usually around 10 a.m. I use the time between 10 a.m. and 12:30 p.m. to create, write, and edit. I use the "pomodoro method." Set a timer for 25 minutes and get to work. Take a five-minute break, and then get right back to another 25 minutes of productive work. Stopping, getting up, drinking water, and moving my body makes a huge difference in my productivity. I rinse and repeat this method for as long as I need to. And the things that require the most focus for me get done in those two to three hours.

I try to take a good, solid break at 12:30 before my afternoon starts. At 1 p.m., I'm back to work. Usually, this is where I hop into my inboxes and post and check back in on social media for comments and inquiries. The rest of the afternoon is spent checking things off my list that I didn't get done earlier, as well as engaging in mentoring calls and teaching.

One of my future goals is to be able to stop working at around 3 p.m. and use the last two hours of my workday to be creative and fuel my soul. I'm not quite there yet, but it's on the horizon. I want to take up painting and I want to learn pottery. Delving into different hobbies for me has been unbelievably beneficial. Find a hobby and work it into your day-to-day routine. This is *creative rest* and our bodies crave it.

I HAVE A SET TIME THAT I WORK EACH DAY.

Discipline has become my way of life. I never fully realized the importance of this until the past year or so. I used to work all the time, thinking that I was accomplishing more. I was always on my phone or computer which just contributed to my avalanche of problems. Work was causing my burnout and I never considered turning it off. At some point, you have to realize that it's time to close the computer, Friend! Because when you are healing from burnout, you have to complete the cycle in order to move on. If the computer never closes, that whole cycle stays open. And so does your state of burnout. Think of it as that little spinning circle you see on your screen when you download or open a program on your phone or computer. You see the circle spinning, but until it fully finishes, you can't do anything.

Work was my major source of burnout and I just never shut it off, so I stayed right where I was. Now, closing my computer and all the apps on my phone at the end of the day completes that cycle for me. It makes a massive difference. Sometime between 3 and 5 p.m. each day, I stop working. I close my computer, mute my apps, and I check out. It's absolutely liberating!

I HAVE A DESIGNATED PLACE WHERE I WORK EVERY DAY.

I know what some of you are already thinking. *"Well, that's a luxury that I don't have."* But that's not true. You don't need to have a designated office. In fact, for over a year, we lived in an RV and my office was a tiny desk and chair in my daughter's bedroom. We all can make a designated place where we work each day. Maybe it's a corner of a room, the kitchen table, anywhere that says it's time for work—*and this does not mean your bed*. Without a valid reason, working from bed is a big no-no. You need a place where your computer stays and also gets shut down at the end of the day. And along the same lines, I do not endorse moving your computer from room to room, unless there is a specific and purposeful reason.

I CREATED MY NON-NEGOTIABLES.

Before I had boundaries, I worked all the time. I never took time off, I worked on my kids' birthdays, holidays, etc., and I missed so much with my friends and family because I told myself the lie that "I have to do this to be successful." But this was simply *not* true.

You are the CEO and you get to make the decisions. Not your clients. At the beginning of the year, sit down with your calendar and mark off dates that you will not work *and stick to it*. This is a big step toward taking back control of your business, Friend.

Here are some non-negotiables for me in my business:

- I take two days a week where I have no client work—just time for me to work on my business.

- I don't book any work for clients in the months of August, December, and January. I can still work on my business with limited hours but no calls, mentoring, or shoots.

- I don't work weekends when I am at home and not traveling. I try to follow this rule as much as I can when traveling too.

- Unless I have a deadline, I start work by 9 a.m. and end work between 3 and 5 p.m.

- I schedule creative time during my workday.

I ADDED "TIME-OFF" TO MY SCHEDULE FOR REST.

Friend, taking time for rest is not a waste of time. Our bodies are not created to constantly be in a state of work. I no longer work weekends. I know that is not possible for everyone, but if you do have to work weekends, pick a day of the week and don't work at all. Even God rested on the seventh day. Do you think maybe He was trying to tell us something? I certainly do. Our minds need a reset. So, take naps or go for walks in nature, alone or with someone you want to give your time to. Play with your pet, read a book, watch a movie, or do crafts. Just stop working all the time. Shut down and turn off those electronics. This has been monumental for my healing. I no longer feel guilty about setting up those boundaries. I need rest to be my best.

I LISTEN TO MY BODY OVER EVERYTHING ELSE.

For the majority of my life, I neglected my body and my health in my race to be successful. Today, I'm paying for it. I now live with a chronic autoimmune illness that could one day take away my ability to walk. I have anxiety and depression, which is mostly under control, but it will never go away completely. I live daily with something called adrenal fatigue because my body lived in a state of survival mode for way too many years. For me, to get up and function daily is not always an easy task. Most days, I'm okay because I'm healing, but some days, not so much. Most of the time I can push through, but some days I cannot, and I no longer beat myself up for that.

If I'm tired, I sleep. If I feel overwhelmed, I take a break and then go back to it later. My body keeps the score for me now. I listen and connect with it often throughout the day. I no longer push myself to my limits. I've already been there and I've got the oversized T-shirt, to boot. I'm 51 years old, and I'm planning on living for many more trips around the sun. But not if I neglect my body. I was so tired of just surviving. Now I want to *live*.

TO WRAP THIS CHAPTER UP . . .

Focusing on your self will allow you to clear all the clutter away and begin to see the picture behind the debris. Because when I started putting my self first, this is what happened:

- I kissed burnout goodbye permanently because I figured out how to avoid it.

- I found a deeper sense of purpose.

- I found joy in my work again.

- I found new inspiration to make my business successful in a healthy way.

- I wake up every single day excited to live a full life.

And even if you don't see it yet, it's right there. I could almost point it out for you, but you have to be the one who discovers it. Discovering what your *self* needs on your own is enlightening, inspiring, encouraging, essential, and spiritual.

So now, let's have you put your thoughts to paper for your own menu of ideas to incorporate into your daily life. At first, it won't be everything that you need to do, but it will open the gates so things can begin falling into place. When that happens, you'll see more possibilities.

What are your production priorities that *must* be on your schedule? How much time do you realistically need for each? It can't just be in your head. Listen to *yourself* and write it down.

_____

_____

_____

_____

_____

_____

_____

_____

_____

_____

_____

_____

_____

S = Self

Now put those production priorities into a logical order for each portion of your day, as well as for your week, and create a routine.

_____

_____

_____

_____

_____

_____

_____

_____

_____

_____

_____

_____

_____

_____

S = Self

What are some non-negotiables that would improve your business and your life? Be honest with yourself and don't hold back.

_____

_____

_____

_____

_____

_____

_____

_____

_____

_____

_____

_____

_____

_____

_____

S = Self

What kind of rest will allow you to keep your responsibilities at a healthy distance while still allowing you to be productive?

_____

_____

_____

_____

_____

_____

_____

_____

_____

_____

_____

_____

_____

_____

_____

_____

S = Self

What are some things that your body is trying to tell you?
Listen carefully for them and write them below.

_____

_____

_____

_____

_____

_____

_____

_____

_____

_____

_____

_____

_____

_____

_____

_____

S = Self

Okay, this chapter had a lot going on, contrasting between some intentional depth and some lighter, basic strategies to help you structure your mental approach to the responsibilities of your work life. Now, take a break and go be *you* for a little while. Go get some ice cream or put on some music and dance like nobody's watching. The remainder of this book will still be here for you when you come back. And I promise, it will be fun.

PART 2:
CHAPTER 3

U = UNITY

Looking back on it, I am able to see that for so many years, I did what I thought I needed to do in order to survive. In my current frame of mind, I am able to say with humility that what I believed were survival techniques were actually naïve approaches to a certain level of balance and stability that I desired. I mistakenly assumed that survival hinged on the abundance of financial resources because it's easy to believe that money can pave the road for all your decisions. But it can't. At least not in the way we customarily view things.

Most of us look at survival merely as the ability to stay alive. We think that anything that prolongs our existence from one moment to the next is good. And, in turn, we believe that good things are supposed to bring us happiness. So, it's no wonder that society at large has always equated financial stability with happiness.

Of course, financial stability is important because society expects us to pay our own way. In fact, there are entire systems in place to prevent access to privileges unless you are willing to pay the required amount. Just try getting on a plane without a ticket and you'll see very quickly that you can't even make it to the security gate because you haven't paid for the privilege. So yes, financial stability is important, but to think all your decisions should be based on accumulating more is myopic. Financial success allows you to take on a greater variety of decisions, but you need to have a determined, internal sense of personal unity and make your decisions based on developing your *emotional stability*. All of your decisions and actions should support precisely this.

When we build our success based on what we see others doing, commonly referred to as "keeping up with the Joneses," we will eventually burn out. The fact is, we have no idea what the Joneses are going through on a personal level. They might appear to have the best of everything, but they might also be coming apart at the seams because they are making decisions that don't unite their sense of self with their sense of completeness. The right kind of success can only be achieved if all the moving parts are aligned with our core beliefs and morals.

For me, in my drive to be the best, and to prove to everyone that I was good enough (and of course, be all and please all), I grossly underestimated the importance of my emotional state of mind. If I am being completely honest, I disregarded it altogether. My decisions did not align with my intended outcome. I ignored the value of my inner being and placed all the value on financial growth. There was no unity in my pursuit of success. Julie wasn't part of the things I had accumulated and they weren't part of me. It was all just extra baggage.

When you go through something hard and you have nothing to give anymore, that's when you find out the truth. And as hard as it is, you have to let things go to fully align. You can't be one way in your personal life and one way in your business life. There needs to be unity in both of them. I am ashamed of myself for all the times that I climbed that ladder and forgot who I really was. I sacrificed my beliefs, my family, and my true friends for fame and money. The three most important things in my life were sacrificed for awards, titles, and for people that dropped me like a hot potato the moment things got hard for me and I had to step away. I hadn't built a foundation upon which to grow and develop my character. No, I had built a spring-loaded trap that closed on me when I trusted in a system for financial gains' sake. I would tell myself, "More is better. More brings happiness. More is *more*." But as soon as that trap closed, I realized that "more" could actually be less than nothing at all if it's the result of haphazard prioritizing.

So, let's do some work. Using the following pages, I want you to make a comprehensive list of all the things you do currently in your day-to-day life and business. And when I say a comprehensive list, I mean *everything* you do, right down to answering emails, making lunches for the kids, or even cleaning toilets. I call this "brain dumping." The reason for this is that there's a lot you do every day, seemingly on autopilot. You don't really *think* about doing them. You just do them without considering how they affect you.

After you write them out, go back and put a star next to the ones that bring you joy and bring unity to align with your present and future life. Then go back through the list again and put an X beside the things you do that add stress to your life or steal your time. These are the things that take from your well-being. Also make note of the things you do daily that don't directly bring you money because they are the things you could outsource. Time is money and I promise you that giving up money to have more time will actually help you make more money. (I know, I know—sounds impossible but just trust me on this.)

Save this list and keep adding to it. We are going to come back to it later.

_____

_____

_____

_____

_____

_____

_____

_____

_____

_____

_____

_____

_____

_____

_____

_____

_____

PART 2:
CHAPTER 4

C = COMMUNITY

Okay, so now we are onto something a little less obvious, but significantly important all the same. I don't care who you are or who you think you are, but NO ONE has earned success without the help of others. Sure, you might have done all the hard work to get to whatever stage you are at, but do you think all those grand ideas and the return on them just came to you out of nowhere? Nope. Nice try, though. You have been inspired and have learned from others.

One of my biggest pet peeves in my beloved photography industry is when people gain fame or popularity and never give credit to their mentors who have helped them get to where they are.

The fact is, someone else played a part in your success too. You have most certainly read a book, followed a pro on YouTube, taken a class, attended a workshop, or been a part of a mastermind event at some point that led you in the direction of your current situation. By default, this means that every single one of us is using some tool in our business that we learned from someone else. It has always been, and will always be, a community that makes us who we are today. Yes, I know, we all have personality traits that filter our incoming information and how we respond to it. And you may even be able to discern between fleeting thoughts and high-density input—choosing what to pay attention to and how to sift through it. But as the saying goes, "There is nothing new under the sun." Every single person around you knows something you don't. About life, about love, about God, faith, family, relationships, success, technical things—you name it.

If you want true success, you must have community. And you need to be willing to build a community that respects every aspect of the community and its members. The good news is, you've already been "interviewing" people your whole life, just with daily exposure to them. I'm sure there are people who you know very well and others not so much. Whatever the depth of each relationship may be, there is plenty to draw from, as well as plenty to share in the form of giving back. So, prepare to do some interviewing of people that you know as well as those you may not know just yet. Keep in mind that a true interview goes both ways. That's why the word is spelled inter-view. It's a two-way flow of perspectives.

There are two main things to keep in mind when approaching this step. First, *be who you are*. Second, *take yourself as seriously as the person you are talking with*.

That little epiphany came just as I knew I needed to accomplish three things. It turns out that those three things became the biggest factors in my healing. I needed to:

- Hire an assistant

- Hire a coach

- Join a mastermind

In getting down to brass tacks on it, it was sad to admit that, on paper, I couldn't really afford any one of them. But, then again, almost in the same breath, I couldn't afford *to not* have them if I was going to move forward. So, I took deep breaths for a couple days, had a few conversations, and I just knew. Humans are not meant to be alone. We need people in our lives to help us. That was one of my biggest mistakes that led to my burnout because I wouldn't ask for help.

Find your tribe, Friend. Build your community of reciprocal respect and set goals for yourself and each other together. Invest in that mastermind. Do your digging. Make sure the coach or the mastermind aligns with you. Just do it. Seek out that coach you think you cannot afford. The rewards of your efforts, as long as you have mindful intent, will meet you down the path you are already walking. And every once in a while, look up and give thanks.

Lately, a number of bees have been showing up at my window and around the outside of my house. Not swarms, just gatherings. They are just flying around and then setting down on leaves and flowers. Interestingly, bees are a well-recognized symbol of community. I can't help but feel it's a little ironic that this is happening around me as I have been writing this chapter. Is it a sign? Yes, it is. It's another one of God's winks to me.

I did a little Google search when I first saw the bees and learned that they are all about community. They do not work alone. A single bee cannot produce honey on its own. There needs to be a hive to have a honeycomb. Those bees are, quite literally, running a little factory and their product is esteemed by nearly every culture around the world. It has medicinal properties. It has therapeutic properties. It makes many things taste better, if that's what you want. It can be quite expensive if you want the "good stuff." But here's the best part! Genuine honey made by bee colonies never goes bad. Let that sink in for a minute.

They have a God-given sense of community, which they contribute to the world, allowing us to learn a little something from them. And so, I say again, a single bee cannot make honey on its own. Neither can we.

With that, let's take a little break. It's time to reflect and do some writing of your own.

_____

_____

_____

_____

_____

_____

_____

_____

_____

_____

_____

_____

_____

Who is a coach or mentor that you would love to learn from?

_____

_____

_____

_____

_____

Are there team members that you could hire that would help your business grow without causing more stress on you? List them here.

_____

_____

_____

_____

_____

_____

_____

_____

_____

_____

_____

_____

Now go back and read your lists, and set a task list to learn more or reach out and connect. Don't view others in your industry as competition. Start that community and build that team. Life is better when we let others in.

PART 2:
CHAPTER 5

C = CLARITY

Have you ever taken a sincere moment to reflect on some deep truths that are exclusively about *you*? You, as in that inner-self we talked about earlier. I mean, there are things that you know, like your neighborhood, basic math, birthdays of people you care about, etc. But then there are things you *really* know. Things like your instincts, your positive and negative triggers, and your conscience.

More often than you might think, in day-to-day conversation with others, people say things like, "I just *knew* I had to (do something)." Or, "As soon as I heard, I just *knew* that (something)." And there is always some kind of emphasis on the word "knew."

No, really! The next few times you go out to a restaurant or an event, listen for that sentence. It's kinda fun. It may come in various forms, but when you hear someone speak that way, you can understand that they are speaking from their inner-self. In reality, when you *know* something at that level and are willing to say it out loud for others to hear, you are revealing your own trust in *your-self*.

Let that sink in.

Along those lines, I am happy to reveal to you that, somehow, I just *knew* that if I was going to get out of this cycle of people-pleasing and stop living my life based on the other people's definition of success, I was going to have to sit down and go deep into some serious work on my character. I *knew* I could not continue as before. I had reached the point of no return and had suffered complete burnout. At the same time, I also knew that I needed to come to a complete stop in order to start over. In essence, the fuse needed to be fixed so the lights could come back on, because I needed clarity to move forward.

Sometimes clarity begins with trusting your gut. In many ways, at that stage of my collapse, trusting my gut was entirely new to me. I had never really listened to *my self* on any kind of impressively deep occasion before. I had always listened to those around me, shaping my mind. I always walked away from that girl in the mirror. But, somehow, I just *knew* that she would come back to visit someday. But this time, I would allow her to stay as long as she wanted *me* to. I've already made up my spare bedroom for her. She is always welcome and I want to spend the rest of my life getting to know her better. I just wish I had had the clarity to grasp on to those moments when they were at hand years ago.

Discovering that was probably the most honest I ever became with myself. I honestly feel like that was one of the hardest but most important steps for me on my road to recovery. And I know this chapter is short by comparison to other chapters in the book, but when things become "clear," they don't really need a lot of explanation. And somehow, I just know that you will be able to look into *your self* and see with clarity the person you always wanted to become. Like all truly great things in life, it will come in time.

In the past, I had always acted upon things because they felt right in that moment or they seemed popular and desirable or trendy. It seldom, if ever, revolved around sitting down and really searching and asking God for clarity. And then I realized that what I really needed was to find a true clarity between God and my self. Or, perhaps a little more accurately,

I needed to pay closer attention to what God was conveying to me. And, please pardon the reference to photography, it's like the images were all there but everything was out of focus. Or like I was only seeing the RAW files that hadn't been edited yet.

As someone who was now beginning to see the volume of self-reflection needed, this was not the time to bring in outside opinions. Nope, this one was personal.

My relationship with God depended on *my* ability to apply the tools and lessons I have acquired through all of this. If I wanted clarity, I had to sharpen my focus without the influence or interference from others. And there was no way I was going to let this change of circumstances revolve around money for anything other than what we really needed to pay our bills.

So we cut back, quite a bit actually, because I needed to shift my focus on making just enough money to meet our needs, while at the same time, I was on this search for clarity in my life and in my business.

Weddings were a big money maker, but weddings often come with a lot of baggage, both physically and psychologically, and were a major contributor to my burnout. I just knew that I had to quit doing them.

And when I finally made that decision, it was like *poof!* Clarity, herself, had just entered the room and shined light on what I felt *led* to do. Despite the fact that this decision created a financial earthquake for us, I knew that if I didn't leave this part of my business, I would never recover. So, I haven't gone back.

I learned that sometimes, we need to sacrifice something and be uncomfortable about it for a while in order to find clarity and embrace it.

Which brings me to how I suddenly found the clarity that I needed on my first truly momentous decision in a long time. It was the one that gave me insight into what I was supposed to do for the rest of my life.

I had to be still.

I had to just sit. I had to get rid of all the noise in my life. I had to sign off of social media. I had to be alone with myself and my thoughts. I needed *me time*, and I knew that I had to talk to Julie, because Julie was talking with God better than I had been up to that point.

From an organizational point of view, I'm all about the lists. I have stacks and stacks of notebooks and I never throw them away. To the average viewer, it may look like a small city built out of paper and boxes, but it's *beautiful*. One day, my grandkids will look through these stacks and think that I was either a genius or someone on the other end of the spectrum.

But back to the point, I'm hoping that you use this book to find *your* clarity. That you come back to these chapters and see your own writing filling these pages, rather than finding an empty notebook. And if you haven't done so already, I want you to go back to that list of all the things you do in your life and business right now. It's literally only a few pages back. Look that over.

They say that most millionaires have about 7 streams of income. Some of them are significant, some not. Maybe all of this will help you focus on the things that bring you fulfillment.

So please, go back and take a hard look over your list and ask yourself if you want to continue doing that particular thing in your life. If you do, circle it. Then I want you to start a new list. This is your future list.

Make a list of all the things that you would love to do *someday*, like your bucket list, even if it doesn't have anything to do with your current business. Consider the multitude of new ways you can take what you are doing now and make it better to free up the time you need to explore and create. New opportunities, new businesses—the possibilities need to be regarded as *endless*.

Clarity

PART 2:
CHAPTER 6

E = ENJOYMENT

As the expression goes, "Doing what you love is freedom. Loving what you do is happiness."

To this day, there is some controversy over who said it first. Some say it was Sudha Murty, who is still alive, while others say it goes back to ancient times. As for me? Maybe I first read it in a fortune cookie! Who knows?

It doesn't matter who said it first. What matters is the meaning behind the message because there's quite a lot going on there.

So, let's rewind a few chapters to part one, where I was describing my burnout. Looking back at the string of events leading to my breaking point, I really had no option other than to firmly believe that I had reached that horrible depth because I no longer enjoyed what I was doing.

My mind had to cut away from it, so I deemed it "undesirable." I would say it was bittersweet in a number of ways but it was just so very *necessary*. And because it was *that* necessary, I just had to be right. *Right?* Well, I was about to learn a few big lessons and see things in a whole new perspective.

When I first started photography, it brought me such enormous joy. Practicing an art, especially professionally, is quite a rush. And a good rush is very easy to get addicted to. So, I worked a lot because I loved it *that* much. But sometimes, you don't know when the thing you love is taking a lot from you. That thing you love is controlling your schedule, your mind, your heart, and basically your life. And over the years, I noticed that things started shifting. At the end of 2019, I started resenting the career that had once brought me so much joy.

But, as usual, I had convinced myself that I had no choice but to continue with this life-sucking, spirit-draining collage of issues. All of the enjoyment of my profession, that part of my life which occupied way more of my time than my entire family, was almost entirely gone. The little bit that was left was both shallow and circling the drain. But I pressed forward anyway, while ignoring the warning signs that were already clearly on display. And as a result, I found myself sitting on the bathroom floor two years later with a pile of pills in my hand because I felt that it was the only way I could escape.

Without retelling all the unpleasant details of that story, what I'm getting at is that life is too short to keep working in a career that you hate. It can be even worse if it's the *job* that hates *you*. But quitting that job can make life extremely uncomfortable for an unknown period of time, and no one really wants to bring that upon themselves. Especially if they are financially responsible for others. Sadly, too many people have convinced themselves that they simply cannot find enjoyment in their jobs. But Friend, that is just soooo not true.

Personally, I believe you can work just about any job and find a way for joy to come to you. It's really all in the mindset. And during the recovery after my breakdown, I found a way to do exactly that. I think this can help you too.

Now, a couple of very obvious issues should come to mind about where I am going here. The first is security, which comprises all the things that money provides for you. It pays for your food, shelter, clothing, education, etc., and also allows for every imaginable level of quality between basic needs and extreme luxury.

The other issue is fulfillment, which is composed of all your feelings, emotions, sentiments, passions, reactions, etc., and allows for every imaginable level of quality between positive and negative, inspiration and fear, pleasure and pain, joy and misery, excitement and disdain. I could go on, but I think you get the picture.

So, what do most people naturally think of when looking at these two concerns? They think, "Okay, I just need to strike a balance and have as much of both as I can."

But wait! Stop. Hold it right there.

Here's the problem most people have with trying to achieve that so-called "balance." Money is quantifiable while emotions are not. And perhaps we can chalk it up to human nature, but most people will dispense of their feelings far too easily for the lure of quantifiable growth.

As a comparison, it's like pebbles vs. water. Pebbles are quite easy to carry around with you and you always know how many you have. If you drop them, you can easily pick them back up, count them to make sure you haven't lost any, and continue on your way.

Water, on the other hand, is very different. For one thing, you need some kind of a storage container. And even then, if you spill some of it, or all of it—ha! Good luck picking it back up.

You see, we count money in dollars, pesos, yen, francs, rupees, etc. Heck, we even arrange it all into separate piles we call "accounts" for budgeting and investment purposes.

Emotions, however, are totally different. You can't count them in terms of "one happiness, two happiness, three happiness" and so on, because it doesn't work that way. And we can't put them into accounts the same way we can with money.

We view our emotions in terms of hours, days, weeks, months or years of happiness, sorrow, fun, boredom, pain, anxiety, joy or *whatever*. And when you take a step back and look at this way, you get to see the bigger picture that compels you to identify the sources of those emotions. For example, if you're looking at a photograph way up close, you see hundreds of pixels in the image, but you can't really see the image. From a little further away, you can see an image emerge from the pixels, but you can't really see the pixels. So, you need to develop the ability to keep everything at the proper closeness *and* distance, because *that's* where the balance is. That's where the really important things come into focus at the same time. Once you discover that, true enjoyment becomes tangible. And that's what happened to me. But in my case, it became tangible *again*.

So, what will it be? I know we need money to survive. But what are *you* going to do? One thing for sure is that you are going to have to make a few decisions, and then a few more. Keep in mind as well, that not making the decisions you have in front of you is the same as deciding to not make any progress.

Believe me. I know. That's what I did and it led to my inevitable burnout and personal horror story. But when I finally started making those decisions, it made all the difference in the world between being miserable in a life-threatening way and beginning to live a life full of joy.

So, you have to ask yourself if the money is really worth that much to you. If you are able to maintain that high income while also being fulfilled with life and enjoying those around you, then perhaps you've reached an appropriate balance that works for you. But if you haven't reached that point yet, I suggest you consider that sometimes water is more valuable than pebbles.

Because frankly, it doesn't matter how much money you are making. If you don't enjoy it, find another job. Life is just way too short to not love what you do. We should work to live and not live to work. You don't need fancy cars, big houses, or designer clothes and shoes to be truly happy. I had all that and I was still miserable on the inside. Money, by itself, does not automatically bring the enjoyment, happiness, or fulfillment that people believe it promises. In fact, it is often the case that making more and more money merely gives greater reason to spend it foolishly.

Success always requires sacrifice, so you need to decide if what you are giving up is really worth it. Because I can tell you truthfully, no amount of money, fame, or status is worth your life.

Keep it in your mind, as well as in your heart, that when we are living our *true* success based on *our* terms, we will have the enjoyment we are seeking.

And today, I love photography again. I made the conscious decision to set up some major boundaries for myself with my photography business. For example, I only take on projects that bring me joy and I only work with clients who are the right fit. Clients who love and appreciate what I am doing. Clients who respect me and my time. Clients who trust me. Clients who want to connect with me as a person and don't just view me as hired help. I no longer say yes to anything just for the paycheck. I would rather eat homemade peanut butter and jelly sandwiches instead of fine dining any day if it means avoiding clients that steal my joy and detract from my sense of self-worth. I care deeply about what I do and who I work for.

I am an AWESOME photographer and coach. And I don't mean that in a conceited way. Rather, I am saying that because I always put my whole heart into everything that I do on a professional level. But, just as importantly, I put my whole heart into everything that I do on a *personal* level.

And YOU are awesome too. I mean the *real* you, that someone in there who is earnestly seeking your own transformative enjoyment. It's time to find it.

So, let's pause for you to decide what you want to enjoy in life. Write them down. And after you write these things down, start making a few more decisions about incorporating them into your life. I pinky-promise it will go a long way.

_____

_____

_____

_____

_____

PART 2:
CHAPTER 7

S = STILLNESS

Sometimes you just have to have a conversation with the girl in the mirror.

Hey Julie!

Yeah?

What are we gonna talk about today?

Oh, I've got a really good one today. This is going to be one of our "mirror moments." We're literally going to fly without moving. So, strap in. Or not. Your choice. This is going to be quite a flight.

Fly? Flight? What are you talking about? We're fish.

It's a metaphor.

I know, I'm just kidding. You do like your metaphors. Go ahead. Please continue.

I never would have thought of it on my own at the time, but if you had asked me a year before my fiery tailspin how the word stillness, and the nature of its meaning, could be ascribed to meaningful success, I can guarantee you that one of two things would have happened.

Fiery tailspin?

I'm still on the same metaphor, Julie. It's easier than telling the whole story over again. Besides, you know the story as well as I do.

Yeah, I know. Anyway, what were the two things that could have happened?

I was either going to stare at you, completely deadpan in motionless silence or I was going to laugh in your face. A question like that, back then, just would have been outside my mental zip code. At the pace I was going, I didn't have time to consider *doing nothing*!

Uh huh. Is that what you still tell yourself?

No. I try not to anyway. And, well . . . hey, umm . . . I just wanted to say thank you, by the way.

For what?

You know . . . all of it. And still now.

Oh. You're welcome. Thank you too for getting through all that with me. I couldn't have done it without you.

Me neither. Hey . . .

Yeah?

You know, it's nice to talk more often now.

Yeah, it really is. So, what do we do now?

I dunno. Maybe just keep swimming?

Yeah, I kinda like that idea.

So . . . umm . . . what did you learn from, you know, everything we went through?

I think I figured out a question we should have talked about a while ago.

And what's that?

Oh, you know. Things that help.

What kinds of *things* and what kind of *help*?

Oh, you know. The things that matter. Things that help you because they matter. That kind of stuff.

You've been thinking for a while, huh?

Sometimes too much, maybe? Sometimes not enough, I think?

Yeah, but just lying here for so long, you've been able to chill for a while, right?

Yes.

And?

Sometimes all I can do is think. Sometimes all I can do is try to remember. Sometimes I try to not remember.

You know you're going to remember it all, right?

I hope so.

But what you're *really* gonna do is focus on the things that bring you closer to your principles.

I guess that's good advice.

You okay?

I think so. Pretty sure, actually.

Oh, you're fine. Trust me. You're good.

Okay. Got any more wisdom for me?

Do you really want to hear it?

Am I going to like it?

I think so.

Well, I trust you. Go on.

Do you know why you're thinking so much recently while lying here all the time?

One way or the other you're going to tell me, right?

No. We're going to *talk* about it. It'll be fun.

I remember "fun."

What do you remember?

I remember! I remember! P. Sherman! 42 Wallaby Way! Sydney!

Oh, stop it. You're going to make me cry.

I was trying to make you laugh. We've done enough crying for the whole Pacific. But it doesn't hurt as much as it used to, though, does it?

No, it doesn't. You're right. It *has* gotten a lot better. I think *I* have too.

Umm . . . weren't you going to tell me something? You said you thought I would like it.

Okay, but you have to pinky-promise that you won't interrupt this time.

That's going to be hard. You know how hard we always try to out-do each other.

Yeah. But this time we both win. It's about time for us to start winning again. But this time, the right way. Everything will be on our terms, okay? No more tailspins. No more time spent on things that don't bring you deeper satisfaction. Only enjoyment, clarity, unity—stuff like that. But you have to promise me you'll listen all the way through this time.

Okay.

Pinky-promise? C'mon Julie. Pinky-promise?

Okay. Pinky-promise.

Good. Soooooooo, instead of swimming, let's just chill here and be still for a little while.

Don't we have to worry about bigger fish?

Not here. We're good here.

Okay. Go ahead. I promise I'll listen. You were saying?

Okay. Here goes. We started talking about stillness a few minutes ago, and we're being still right here, right now for a reason. I'm going to give you an example of it that you've already experienced, but maybe didn't really grasp when it happened. I think this is really going to help you.

Stillness?

Shhh!

Sorry.

Shhh!!!

Bear with me here. This is going to take a moment, but I promise it'll be worth it.

Okay, think of a time when you woke up on some morning, somewhere between one and two hours earlier than you needed to or even anticipated. And the moment you open your eyes, becoming aware that you are no longer sleeping, you realize that you have not moved any part of your body in the slightest yet, other than your beating heart and two eyelids. You're not truly awake or conscious yet. You're just *aware* that you're not sleeping, but not really aware of anything else. Am I making sense so far?

Kind of?

And then you just kinda stay there—seemingly motionless to everyone and everything, except God and your eyelids. And you don't move a single muscle for a good long moment or two, until you think, "Well, I could go back to sleep, buut thiiis juuuust feeeeels soooooooo goooooooood." Normally, you would just automatically try to go back to sleep without recognizing there was another option available. But *this* time, you remain motionless long enough to be able to physically and subconsciously feel that genuine rest has come upon you—the inner you. And for a little while, there's no way you could even imagine trading that moment for the value of the whole world.

Okay...

That is stillness. It's internal quiet, no matter the volume of your surroundings. And here's the kicker—you didn't find it on your own. No, it found you. And *it* decided that *you* need a tall glass of it every once in a while. Stillness is not rest, or even the act of resting. Rather, stillness is where you can feel yourself resting. It's where you can hear yourself thinking and where you see yourself in the act of being. It may be the closest thing to holy peace you'll ever encounter while your heart is beating on this earth. You can't actually hear it, but it's where silence is deafening, and the sound of thunder could almost be God's footprint being made in real-time, right next to you, without even startling you. And a thought comes to you that stillness may even be the scent of heaven.

Well? You're just going to float there?

I pinky-promised I wouldn't interrupt.

You mean, you were listening?

Every word. Why? Are you going to quiz me?

Little by little.

Where did you come up with all that?

I've been around you for a while. We had it coming.

That was pretty intense.

It's supposed to be.

Wow. Just . . . just . . . wow.

Yeah. I know. Wow. And hey, by the way, you're gonna need more of it on a regular basis if you really want the kind of life you've been writing about in your book. You can't just *tell* people about it. You gotta *do* it too. You're gonna need to put stillness on your schedule. It'll really take you places.

Good to know. I guess you're gonna have to do it as well.

I know. We can work on it a little at a time. Hey, you know, I once heard someone say that "stillness is the altar of spirit."

Yeah, but it's silence, not stillness.

What? You sure?

Yes. Totally sure. But I will tell you this—if silence is the altar of spirit, then stillness is the bed that it rests upon.

Did you just come up with that right here on the spot? Wait . . . who's teaching who here?

It was my turn. I thought I'd chime in a little more. You know, to make sure we get things right for all that we're working on.

Well . . . it's just . . . well, I thought it was pretty clever.

Thank you. And hey . . .

Yeah?

This was fun. Let's go. We can do this again tomorrow. Okay?

Deal. And until then . . .

Just keep swimming.

How do you find stillness?

What questions would you ask the girl in the mirror and how would you reassure her?

_____

_____

_____

_____

_____

_____

_____

_____

_____

_____

_____

_____

_____

_____

_____

_____

PART 2:
CHAPTER 8

S = SATISFACTION

If you don't mind, I'm going to hop back to my earlier examples of mashed potatoes and gravy, pebbles vs. water, and the pixels in the photograph to ask a question. When does too much of one, or not enough of the other, become harmful or destructive?

Well, if you really think about it, the seed-crystal for satisfaction truly begins with having "enough" of something, whatever that something may be. Let's start there.

As an infant and then toddler, your needs for satisfaction are pretty basic and are entirely provided for you. But over time, you begin to voluntarily seek satisfaction on quite a number of highly important fronts. These include your physical and mental health, your body, mind, spirit, soul, heart (the inner one), intellect, and from there they go on to include things like your relationships with God, family, friends, clients, colleagues, advisors, etc. And then they go on to include things like career, finances, freedom, adventure, curiosity, knowledge, skill, creativity, entertainment, fun, and on, and on, and on. These are the things that your life constantly juggles in your reality. But wait, there's more, because then your psyche is telling you that your responsibility is to go look for *all* of them! That's a pretty tall order! The older, and hopefully wiser you become, the more important each of these can become as well. Maybe not all of them at the same time, but certainly a great deal of them much of the time.

Okay, you can take a breath now because I'm going to try to put a bow on this.

Considering everything I mentioned above, this is why you have to pay attention to all the pixels in the image. If you want to concentrate on your marriage—great! If finances are what you really want to focus on—go for it. But it has to be good for the whole and complete **you**. And *that* is why you have to pay attention to the image emerging from the pixels. They always go together and are always integrating with each other at both the micro and macro levels.

I'm sorry to introduce just one more analogy, but I promise this is the last one. You are flying solo, and you have to both *fly* and *navigate* simultaneously. You can't just go on autopilot the whole time. You'll get lost, run out of fuel, then crash and burn, which I really don't recommend. Been there, done that. Not pretty.

So, go back up to the list of items in the second chapter of part two and decide which of these specific items should be added to what you wrote in chapter six on Enjoyment. These two chapters work hand in hand. Then, give yourself a tall glass of stillness and dig a little deeper to add some things that you think up on your own. You'll be amazed by where your mind goes and you might come up with something that is a true gem.

Okay, I can take a breath now too.

I didn't fully realize it as a little girl but I always wanted more. But I'm not talking about money here. No, it was more like youthful ambition. People around me always wanted me to perform, whatever that meant. And okay, I must admit that I did get better at certain things that maybe weren't exactly what gave me satisfaction at the time, but it would be silly for me to be upset at myself for improving at a number of things which are good skills to have anyway, and that also made people I cared about happy. So, of course, I accepted them. And as I grew up, this led to more responsibility, which is generally a good thing to have for your own sense of stability in the world. But even at a very young age, I lived by the notion that if they could do it, so could I. I was constantly searching for the next big idea. I had had so many victories that other people would love to have. And yet, I was always comparing myself to others I didn't know and I could never quite see how good it was at my own doorstep. Sadly, for me, the grass was always greener on the other side.

But in March of 2020, everything changed.

Over the past 3 years, God has really taught me that even when life is hard, I can be satisfied with where I am at this very moment. As a family, we have experienced cancer, death, financial concerns due to COVID, a move, RV-living on the road (still trying to figure that phase out), a pause in our life to become caregivers, a breakdown, walking away from the security of a high-paying career and losing my identity in the process, as well as a huge degree of uncertainty with not understanding the decisions to be made ahead of us.

And even now, my life at the moment, where I am living in Ohio in a rented home, taking care of my mother-in-law, and pivoting my business is NOT the life I envisioned for myself at 51 years old. But I can truly say that I'm satisfied. I'm at peace and completely trusting God to lead us to what is next.

You will never have true success if you can't or won't allow yourself to have satisfaction. And because this realization hit me so hard, I have discovered that it seems to be an inescapable law of the universe. It's okay to have big goals and want to always improve, but first, we need to be able to find satisfaction with where we are right now. Or at least begin trying.

Did you know that's precisely where self-esteem comes from? Really! As I was writing this, I decided to look it up, just to make sure I got it right, and there are actually three types.

- Overly high self-esteem, which means feeling superior to others, is often displayed through arrogance, self-indulgence, and other expressions of entitlement.

- Low self-esteem means feeling inferior to others.

- A healthy self-esteem means "having an accurate and balanced self-view."

Boom, baby! Right there! Healthy self-esteem is having an *accurate* and *balanced* self-view! Wow, I didn't plan *that*. Some parts of this book just seem to be writing themselves!

So, pay attention to your portions, as well as all your pebbles and water. Keep your eyes on both the images *and* pixels in your field of view. All of these things are always revealing *something* to you.

Even if someone had trillions of dollars but still wasn't satisfied, I could look that person in the eye and say, in God's truth, that I have something that they will never have. And in that sense alone, I am wealthier than they will ever be. That is because I have *enough*, and they don't. I have achieved satisfaction.

Now trust me, money in and of itself is not bad and I have big plans on making money and using it for good and to make sure my future is secure. But I refuse to let chasing money in order to feel worthy and enough ever dictate my life again. You can have success and money without it sucking the life out of you.

And remember, you are living the life that you used to pray for. You are living a life that many desire. If you have breath in your lungs, God still has plans for you. Stop striving to be more, to do more, to have more based on anything other than your inner principles. Stop negotiating too much of your precious water for too few additional pebbles. Stop focusing on just the pixels in your reality and examine the bigger picture. Give yourself enough mashed potatoes to fulfill your needs and then add enough gravy to fulfill your wants. Stop living for the definition of success that other people have determined for you and find your own.

I had to learn this the hard way, but right now, the choice is yours. Which path will you take?

How do YOU find satisfaction?

_____

_____

_____

_____

_____

_____

_____

_____

_____

_____

_____

_____

_____

_____

_____

_____

_____

_____

Epilogue

NOVEMBER 9, 2022

Note to self:

It's been a year since I found myself on that bathroom floor in a puddle of tears.

The one who, just a few months before that night, had shot a wedding at the most exquisite and ideal venue in the French Riviera.

The one who just hosted a photography conference a month ago for 300 people. Who smiled and hugged everyone, but had cried herself to sleep so many nights when she was alone.

Don't misunderstand the Julie you were before all this. I shouldn't be sorry for who I was. I just didn't know what I was doing. I know I didn't see it coming. I'm sorry that it took so long. I'm grateful that I survived.

I had "made it" in the photography world. But now I think, *yay*. I represented "the goal" for so many of my fellow photographers. *Yay again*.

All the money. *Whoopie*. All the fame. *Hurrah*. All the publicity, all the mentions, all the hard work. *Fetal position on the bathroom floor*.

Alone. Yes, alone. Congratulations, you reached the top.

But that was then. Now, even though I have recovered as much as I have, I wouldn't trade the lessons I've learned for anything. I have a new perspective on so many individual things, as well as on the big picture. And the focus is so much sharper than ever before. I'm getting my balance back, *real balance*, and I'm getting better at keeping it.

When I was at my darkest, most of those fifty thousand "followers" were nowhere to be found. But that was then! Even my family and closest friends had no idea how bad it really was (and, yeah, I probably still deserve an Oscar). But that was then!

I had no idea who Julie was. I only knew the Julie that everyone else expected me to be. That happy, bubbly, pastel-loving energizer bunny that always said yes to everything. *That* was the Julie that everyone wanted. Not the 9-year-old shy girl with pigtails, who would have rather been reading or listening to music on the record player, dancing by herself in her room while she dreamed of being Cinderella.

But that was then.

Now I am flying solo, without auto-pilot. I am not lost and I am not going to run out of fuel. I get to eat mashed potatoes with the perfect amount of gravy. I know the value of pebbles and water. I see the pixels *and* the image. In the stillness of my soul, I am dancing to music I cannot even hear because life itself is orchestral and vibrant.

My dear friend, as I am writing this, tears are gushing down my face. I can't believe that I was willing to lose everything because all the years of people-pleasing and living my life on their terms had put me in such a dark place with such complete burnout that I literally had nothing left to give. The way that I treated myself was inexcusable. But that's not why I'm sitting here typing all puffy-faced and sniffly-nose with tears on my keyboard and lap, a bunch of saturated tissues on the floor next to my chair. Because you know what happened today?

I got to wake up this morning. Many people in the condition I was in never get that chance again. But I am alive. I am healing. I have changed. This is *now*. And here I am, right now, writing the ending to my first book.

Nine-year-old me would be so proud.

And isn't that what you really wanted for yourself as a kid? To make yourself and others pleased with the real you? Maybe that's why I should have gotten to know that little girl in the mirror way back then. And yet, in a way, without even knowing it at the time, I did give myself a future gift from myself to *my self* that would truly fulfill me.

Because I made a promise to Julie back then that I would write a book one day—something important that I could say was a genuine accomplishment at the personal level. Well, that may have been a whole lot of years ago, but it is my name on this book that I have poured my heart and soul into, and you are holding it right now. I pray that this will change peoples' lives so they don't feel so alone. It has already changed one life—mine. But hey, I had to start somewhere.

But this is not the end. Oh no, my dear friend, *this* is only the beginning. You've graduated, and this is your commencement. It's *your* turn now. *Right now.*

And so, just like Cinderella, I learned through this process that I don't have to become someone else to be seen. The clock may have already struck midnight, but my fairytale has not ended. I still have the other glass slipper which proves I lived through all of those events. I have learned how to become the Julie I was born to be. The people who *truly* matter in my life will love me for being *me* just the way I am.

So now, let's all live our own version of happily ever after. Because deep down, I do believe that fairytales exist. We just need to have the courage to write them ourselves. Stop living everyone else's fairytale, or anyone's but your own. It's not a one-size-fits-all kind of thing. You get to determine your ending. You get to decide what to do with this one big, beautiful life that you have been given. You deserve to be happy in your life and your business. It took me over half a century to realize this, but *you* can start now.

Life is not about merely surviving. Life is about living and giving, learning and growing, being and becoming. But most of all, *loving* the way God intended.

It would only be fitting for me to leave you with one of Disney's best quotes. "Everyone falls down. Getting back up is how you learn how to walk."

And that is just what I did. I got back up. I'm learning to walk again. I am becoming Julie.

And cut. Queue the music. I really thought I was going to end this book with that line. But there's actually one thing left to say now that I am at this stage of recovery and healing. And it has to do with that little 9-year-old me in the mirror.

When I examine all the events that got me here, this whole roller coaster story, all the way to this very moment, it is truly calming to know that she's still with me. With everything I've learned, and knowing that God has been with me the entire time, I now understand that when I look in the mirror, it's actually a two-way glass. I can perceive there's an honest stillness with an internal quiet. And standing there, when I look at *my self*, and all that that means, I can't help but notice that it's actually Little Julie on the other side of the glass, who happens to be looking into her own mirror and seeing *me*. She's *still* there. And she's just hoping that I take care of her and treat her well. I know she's praying for me because I'm still here. I hope she sees that I'm doing my best. She knows I want to say thank you to her every single day. I say it to her in my heart all the time. I found myself again in that little 9-year-old girl who was too scared to be her own person.

Now, every time I look in the mirror, I get to say something that is thunderously meaningful to her. In true Dory-fashion, in a purely silent voice, I tell her, "When I look at you, I'm home."

And to those I'm so incredibly grateful for:

I have always loved writing. In fact, I decided when I was around nine that I was going to write a book one day. But this book is not in your hands solely because of me. In fact, two months ago I almost deleted it, so if it was truly just up to me, there would be no book.

Writing a book like this is not for the faint of heart. In fact, it's my heart that has been cut open for all the world to see as I lie naked on the table. I addressed some dark secrets that I had never told anyone until I started writing this book. It is deep trauma that I only touched on the surface. I wanted to be careful with my words, as to not offend and show respect to those I love. Writing this book was one of the hardest things and ,to be honest, this book was not written with the intent of a bestseller. No, I wrote this book to heal myself and hopefully my story will, in turn, heal others.

The list of thank you's it's long. Here we go.

First of all, *ALL* glory is given to God. Without Him, I am nothing.

To my husband, Matt, you are my opposite in all the right ways and I could not do life without you. Thank you for staying by my side "for better or for worse." We've definitely lived up to that part of our vows. I love you with all my heart. Thank you for trusting and believing in me to write this book without judgment. You are my person. Always. And I love you more.

To my children, Mari-Kate and Noah, you gave me the greatest gift in the world when you called me mama. You have grown into amazing adults and I'm so proud of you both. Love you to the moon and back, forever and ever.

To my parents, thank you for always being there for me and making me feel safe. Even now. My childhood is full of amazing memories and it's all because of you. I love you both so much.

To my grandmothers in heaven. Thanks for being my angels. I know you were with me while I was writing this book. I felt your presence.

To Keira, my coach and publisher. Thank you for believing in me when I didn't believe in myself. I'm so glad God brought you into my life. I hope you know you are stuck with me now. Love you so much, you little firecracker!

To Brian, my editor. I'm forever grateful that you got in my head and figured out my jumbled mess! You helped me put these words to paper. You are a true rockstar!

To Beth, you kept my business going so I could write. You believed in me and pushed me. You let me cry and vent. God knew I needed you. Thank you. I'm forever grateful for that DM you sent me last August. God used you and I can't wait to see what He has in store for us next.

And to my friends, you know who you are, thanks for still being here. My circle is smaller now but I've never felt so loved.

And for all you, my new friends, let's stay that way, okay? If this book has helped you in any way, please send me a DM on Instagram. I would LOVE to hear from you! You are the reason I keep showing up.

ABOUT THE AUTHOR

Julie lives in Nashville, TN with her husband Matt and daughter Mari-Kate. She is now retired from being a wedding photographer but still uses her skills as a photographer by shooting editorials for various magazines, along with selling her art prints and coffee table books of "All the Pretty Places" that she has traveled.

This season of her life finds her embracing the "slow" and finding rest. She spends her days building a new community for "women entrepreneurs who love like Jesus" called "**THE HIVE**". You will still find her traveling to her favorite places in France and the UK while creating coaching and retreats that evolve around rest.

8615f2ca-6c1a-4d15-9818-8a61ae47e2b7R01